THE CHURCH'S MINISTRY TO THE OLDER UNMARRIED

Dr. M. D. HUGEN

THE CHURCH'S MINISTRY TO THE OLDER UNMARRIED

Wm. B. Eerdmans Publishing Company
Grand Rapids, Michigan

PHOTOLITHOPRINTED BY CUSHING - MALLOY, INC.
ANN ARBOR, MICHIGAN, UNITED STATES OF AMERICA

TO MY PARENTS

FOREWORD

I welcome and commend this book by Melvin D. Hugen as a significant contribution to the emerging pastoral theology of our day — fully rooted in the biblical Christian witness, and precisely relevant to the peculiar needs of our time. I respect at all points the integrity of the author's thought, the sincerity and intelligence of his biblical commitment, the fearlessness of his study of the personality sciences, the penetration of his theological method, and the passion of his concern for a group of persons much mistreated not only by our society but also by the churches. As will be noted, there are aspects of his conclusions about which I am doubtful, but the differences between us are only matters of emphasis.

The end-point of action to which our attention is directed is indicated properly in the title of the book. But before we can reconsider the ministry of the church to this group, we need to know the needs and problems of that group. The delineation of this situation constitutes a major contribution.

As soon as we move beyond some such age period as the twenties, then the over-arching fact is that society's "censure of the single woman is unambiguous and forceful." All may not be easy either for the bachelor. But it is the woman unmarried, in the age bracket suggesting she may never marry, on whom society is merciless. A generation or two ago such a woman was thought of by society as "mild, mousy, dull, ineffective, sexless." In that image contempt was at least mixed with pity. Today's image sees such a woman as "emotionally warped, sour, maladjusted, neurotic," and above all "sexually starved." This image contains not even pity, only the modern equivalent of complete outer darkness.

Every unmarried person, especially the woman, who moves into middle life, Dr. Hugen rightly maintains, has to deal with this kind of prejudgment of her by society. And it is a prejudgment, operating precisely like any prejudice. One may know a schoolteacher, physician, nurse, or secretary of middle years who is manifestly none of the things indicated by the stereotype. This person may be exempted from it, but the stereotype remains. And it may be as hard to demonstrate that one's singleness is not necessarily neurotic as it is to demonstrate that another's dark pigmentation does not necessarily make him stupid.

How has this come about? Bad as was the earlier mousy image it is not nearly so evil as the present neurotic image. What has produced the change? Here Dr. Hugen faces the facts unflinchingly. This lies in our growing romanticizing of marriage. By absolutizing marriage as *"the* feminine role in life," we have unwittingly but idolatrously degraded the woman as first human being and child of God. Indeed, we have gone so far as to regard any kind of accomplishment or service by a woman who is unmarried as, at the very best, but a poor substitute.

The biblical account will support no such position. Dr. Hugen courageously, truly, and provocatively asserts that "the coming of Christ has relativized the significance of marriage and parenthood." Goods these may indeed be for many, even most people. But they are not God. They are not absolute. They are not uniformly binding on individuals. A woman's value, he continues flatly and correctly, "is not determined by her marital status." The societal stereotype that would make it so must, by Christians, "be rejected without qualification."

The first and the most important aspect of the church's ministry to the older unmarried must lie in precisely this reassessment of attitudes. Without such reconsideration, even repentance, no action can be relevant and effective. When it comes to specific modes of ministry, the author is wisely cautious. On many things we are ignorant, and here there can be no substitute for our courageous exploration. I find myself more skeptical than the author over the wisdom of church marriage bureaus for those of middle years, however wisely these be administered. And he seems to me more legalistic in some of his recommendations, however tentatively put, than I find myself. The reader should see what I believe the author means. We do not know the precise answer for these people. What we need to do is to explore it with such people in the light of the whole biblical witness on the one hand, and the specific situation of these people on the other. The reader who misses this, perhaps by lighting on some particular point of conduct, misses the whole book.

As very nearly the sole American in this century who has written of "poimenics," I welcome Dr. Hugen to a kind of American Poimenical Fellowship. "Poimen" is the Greek word for shepherd, and "poimenics" is the study of shepherding. Although his treatment of this is brief in its structural sense, it notes rightly, in my judgment, that poimenics transcends any of the special offices of the ministry and, in at least one of its two branches (traditionally called "special poimenics") involves the whole ministry to individual persons.

Poimenics, like every branch of theology, has its roots in the Bible and the gospel and must be aware of this at all times. At the same time, "The investigation of the social and psychic aspects of man and his problems is a legitimate and even essential part of the theological science of poimenics." Without such investigation the study would be incomplete and perhaps irrelevant.

The author rightly denies that such a position necessarily involves naturalism, reductionism, or any form of humanism. It does deny that the ministry of the church to the person is wholly limited to the "personal proclamation of the Word." For God's revelatory Word may in some sense appear in many realms of life, including the social and psychological studies. Alertness to such possibilities, always guided by the biblical witness of course, affirms God's activity in relation to the whole of life.

A study of this kind has direct practical consequences and implications, even though we should be cautious about drawing too specific conclusions in view of the complexity of the subject and the weight of our ignorance of it. But the study leads also to a reconsideration of the gospel bases, in interpenetrating relationship with the complex data of psychology and sociology. Thus it contributes toward an improved pastoral theology.

Carried on in Amsterdam as this study was, its omission of reference to some of the relevant studies by Americans in pastoral theology and pastoral psychology is understandable. The author is to be encouraged to continue his work along this line. His further utilization of the additional materials available will further strengthen the basis of the important thesis he sets forth here.

I should value Dr. Hugen's study very much even if a large number of our respective theological convictions were different. It is additionally gratifying to find myself in agreement with him on so many aspects of understanding our common Christian faith.

—SEWARD HILTNER
Professor of Pastoral Theology

The University of Chicago
March 1960

CONTENTS

Chapter I

INTRODUCTION

Chapter II

THE SOCIAL PROBLEM OF THE OLDER UNMARRIED

Chapter III

THE PERSONAL PROBLEMS OF THE OLDER UNMARRIED

Chapter IV

THE SPECIFIC FORMS OF THE CHURCH'S MINISTRY
TO THE OLDER UNMARRIED

PREFACE

For twenty-two years, a quarter of a lifetime, my parents have afforded me an education. They have supported me, encouraged me, trusted me, and prayed for me; they have molded my person and given me direction. Few have cared and done so much.

Sylvia is one of those few. For five years she has been the wife of a student—to those who have been students, this says enough.

Many others have given their aid: the family of my wife, my brothers and sister, and many friends. My fellow American students have helped shape my thinking and my life. They have introduced me to much modern thought in areas of theology other than my own. They have shown Christian love and service. These need special mention: David Holwerda and Philip Holtrop, for reading my thesis and for their profitable comments, and Marie Holtrop, Joel Nederhood, and John Primus, for spending many tedious hours reading proofs.

The Free University of Amsterdam has introduced me to modern Calvinistic thought: related to the modern world and to modern problems. The carefully exegetical theology of Prof. G. C. Berkouwer, the courageously Biblical ethics of Prof. R. Schippers, and the thoroughly developed psychology of Prof. J. Waterink will always influence my thought. The theological faculty of the Free University has provided the material for solid construction upon a foundation laid well by Calvin College and Seminary.

Of all my mentors none has molded me more than Prof. J. H. Bavinck, my promotor. Through his extensive learning, his substantial wisdom, and his gentle but firm control of my enthusiasm and theological impetuosity, he has shown me the breadth and the depth of the Church's ministry.

CHAPTER I

INTRODUCTION

Theological Foundation

This thesis presupposes the Reformed view of poimenics as defined by Abraham Kuyper in his *Encyclopaedie der Heilige Godgeleerdheid* [1] and further developed in the writings of T. Hoekstra, J. Waterink, J. H. Bavinck, G. Brillenburg Wurth, and J. G. Fernhout. The goal of the ministry of God to the individual through the church [2] is seen, therefore, as the restoration or promotion of a life of reconciliation to

---

[1] Kampen, J. H. Kok, 1909, second edition, Vol. 3, pp. 524—553.

[2] The phrase "the ministry of God to the individual through his church" or, what will be used interchangeably, "the church's ministry to the individual" is employed in this thesis to describe that activity of God through his church, of which poimenics is the science. The term traditionally used in Reformed theology, "care of souls," (a translation of the Dutch *zielzorg* or the German *Seelsorge*) was avoided because of its Pietistic connotations. The word "soul" has come to be used in the dualistic sense of an isolated part of man. The influence of various forms of dualism from Gnosticism through 17th century Pietism and down to the modern form propagated by a separation of science and religion has robbed this term of its Biblical, comprehensive meaning. A beginning of the restoration of the original meaning is being made in modern theology as a result of the growing recognition of the unity of man expressed in the Scriptural use of the word "soul," but this change is much more evident in Europe than in America, the area to which this thesis is oriented. The dualistic connotation of this word, which is still general in the American world, makes its use inadvisable.

The term commonly used in America, "pastoral care," was also rejected since it is too restricted to describe that ministry of which poimenics is the science. It refers to the activity of the special offices of the church and excludes that activity which is the duty of all Christians rising from the universal office of believer, the mutual concern for the welfare of others, described in Col. 3 : 16, 17. The inclusion of this ministry of all believers is very important because especially with such problems as the one dealt with in this thesis, little can be done by the elder, the deacon, and the pastor apart from the congregation as a whole. More generally, the ministry of God through his church is nowhere in Scripture limited to or represented as primarily the concern of the special offices. On the contrary, there are many passages which emphasize the duty of the whole church to minister God's salvation to the needy. Cf., e.g., Col. 3 : 12—17, Rom. 12 : 13, I Cor. 12 : 21, 22, and I Thess. 5 : 11. Therefore, any term used to designate God's ministry to the individual through his church which limits the activity to one or more of the special offices, is a misnomer.

The word "ministry" is used in this thesis in the sense of *diakonia* (Cf., e.g., II Cor. 11 : 8) and is not limited to the preaching activity of one of the special offices. It includes all those acts of service which promote the Christian life and

1

God through faith in Jesus Christ which is directed according to the revealed will of God and devoted to his service. [3] Unto this goal God ministers his Word to the individual through the services not only of the special offices of minister, elder, and deacon, but also of all other believers by virtue of their universal office. Poimenics is the theological science of this ministry of God.

The principle that God works organically in this ministry is a *sine qua non* for a thorough science of poimenics. [4] That principle has two aspects. First, God uses means to accomplish this goal: earthly, temporal, causal means. He uses his written Word, his church, and her offices. Secondly, the man who is the object of this ministry is organically involved. His physical, psychic, and social conditions are utilized by God since they affect his reaction to the gospel.

The progression of this new life is not the mechanical production of a divinely activated machine but the growth of a tender plant from a divinely created seed which needs care and cultivation. The means used by God are not tools or instruments. These terms are too mechanical to express the relationship between God and the means or services involved in the accomplishment of his purpose on earth. Paul's succinct description of this relationship in I Corinthians 3 : 5—9 outlines its organic nature. Paul was opposing an ancient form of naturalism in the early Corinthian church, the party spirit, which focused upon the human servant to the exclusion of the divine giver. Paul said of himself and Apollos οὔτε ἐστί τι, neither is anything. Yet this categorial, direct, objective denial, expressed by the negative ὀυ, does not prevent him from saying in verse nine, we are θεοῦ συνεργόι because I have planted and Apollos has watered. The work done by human servants in the initiation of the new life and in its promotion is as much involved in the production of this life of reconciliation as that of the farmer in planting and cultivating his crop is involved in the production of grain. To call these factors indispensable is no overstatement—nor a reintroduction of Pelagianism. Paul, the propagator of the truth of salvation by grace alone, steadfastly maintained the significance of human activity in the realization of this salvation. God will save everyone who calls upon his name, but how can they call upon him in whom they have not believed, and how are they to believe if they have never heard, and how are they to hear without a preacher? [5] The recognition of God as the

are a consequence of it. This is the sense in which it is commonly used in the terms "the social ministry of the church," "the minstry of music," and "the ministry of religious education."

[3]   J. G. Fernhout, *Psychotherapeutische Zielzorg*, doctor's thesis, Free University of Amsterdam, 1950, p. 81. See also pp. 53—55.

[4]   The following analysis of this principle is based in part upon J. Waterink's development of it in chapter three of *Plaats en Methode van de Ambtelijke Vakken*, Zutphen, Nauta, 1923, pp. 129—193.

[5]   Rom. 10 : 13, 14.

only Savior does not cancel the significance óf human service. The passage in I Corinthians cited above yields this further description of the organic relationship. Though man's work may in a limited, finite sense be called causal, it is God who produces and promotes this new life. [6] Man's work is not causal in the chemical-physical sense of certain conditions invariably producing certain effects. The results are never humanly predictable because they do not automatically produce the life; it is a creation of God. The results are from God, not from man. But man is inseparably involved. He is a co-laborer, συνέργος; what he does and how he does it is of tremendous importance. And yet after all these elements are traced out, the relation of God's activity and man's remains a mystery. The existence of this relation, however, is a reality, known through faith. Both the doctrine of providence and that of the organic ministry of God are concerned with this relation. Just as the former must be defended against denials of God's activity, so the latter against denials of man's, [7] even though the relation between the two remains a mystery. The ministry of the Word through preaching and man's believing response to this Word are as much a part of the mystery of Christianity as are the incarnation and the ascension. Paul says, "And without controversy great is the mystery of godliness." [8] That salvation has come, that men revere and worship God is unexplainable. [9] And significantly, when Paul further defines the content of this mystery, he refers not only to the revealed truths of the incarnation and the ascension and the activity of the Holy Spirit, but also to the human service of preaching and the human response of faith. They are part of the mystery out of which godliness results. [10]

Just as God did not employ male stenographers to record his revelation but produced the Holy Scriptures through organic inspiration, which utilized the individual author's personality, his knowledge, his insights, his history, and his abilities; just as the church is the fruit of God's organic activity in history utilizing nations and kings, peace and wars, victories and defeats; just as dogma is the reflection of revelation through the human mind in such a way that particular men, times, and civilizations at their various levels of development are utilized

---

[6] I Cor. 3 : 7.

[7] Cf. G. C. Berkouwer, *De Voorzienigheid Gods*, Kampen, J. H. Kok, 1950, p. 195.

[8] I Tim. 3 : 16.

[9] The word *eusebeia* is used in the Bible as an act or attitude of man, not as an abstraction referring to Christianity as a system of truths. See J. H. Thayer, *A Greek-English Lexicon of the New Testament*, New York, American Book Company, 1889, p. 262.

[10] "De zakelijke inhoud van het μυστήριον is blijkens de zes volgende regels Christus *en het heil* [italics mine — M. H.], door Hem gewrocht en nu in de zijnen ondanks de tegenstand tot zegepraal gebracht." C. Bouma, *De Brieven van den Apostel Paulus aan Timotheus en Titus*, Amsterdam, H. A. Bottenburg, 1946, from the series, *Kommentaar op Het Nieuwe Testament*, edited by S. Greijdanus, F. W. Grosheide, and J. A. C. van Leeuwen, p. 147.

in this activity of the Spirit; so the ministries of God are accomplished through the organic utilization of human service. Therefore, just as this principle of the organic activity of God is important for the exegetical sciences in the interpretation of the Word, for the ecclesiological sciences in the interpretation of the history of the church, and for the dogmatical sciences in the understanding of dogma, so it is important for the sciences of the various ministries of God through the church. The ministry to the individual, and poimenics as the science of this ministry, may not ignore these human, temporal, historical services involved in this ministry. An understanding of the characteristics, prejudices, abilities, and social adaptability of these servants is vitally necessary for effective and efficient service. Why else does Timothy say that an elder must be socially acceptable, "above reproach," and "well thought of by outsiders"; have a stable, well-developed personality, "temperate, sensible, dignified," "not violent but gentle, not quarrelsome"; be sociable and amiable, "hospitable"; and have good family relations, managing "his own household well, keeping his children submissive and respectful in every way"? [11] In the same chapter he says substantially the same of deacons and in verse thirteen he states explicitly the reason: "For those who serve well as deacons gain a good standing for themselves and also great confidence in the faith which is in Christ Jesus": through these virtues they provoke a favorable response to the gospel.

Secondly, this organic activity of God means that the man who is the object of this saving work of God is totally and personally involved in the process. God saves each man by person and name, not by number. He redeems each man in, through, and according to his personality, environment, history, and society.

This aspect of God's organic activity is clear already in the Old Testament when God presents the gospel of salvation to the people of Israel couched in the hygenic, social, and economic as well as the obviously religious and moral statutes of the *Torah*. These seemingly mundane matters are intimately connected with reconciliation with God. They are not a separate realm that stands in an external relation to the religious realm, but together they form one whole. All these aspects of life are interwoven with the religious aspect. Though a certain distinction can be made between these moral, social, economic commands of God and the *specifically* religious commands, as is done when the law is divided into the first table of loving God above all and the second table of loving one's neighbor as oneself, they are indivisible and basically both religious.

These commands are religious, that is, aspects of man's relation to God, not only because God's salvation is comprehensive of the whole of life—a point that will be discussed later—but because disturbance in

---

[11] I Tim. 3 : 2—7.

these various sociological and psychological areas affects man's religious development and attitudes. Isaiah, for example, says that even a basic instinct like hunger influences the spiritual life: "when they are hungry, they will be enraged and will curse their king and their God." [12] The situation is no different in the New Testament. These aspects are still matters of religious concern. The multitude of admonitions given by Paul and the other apostles concerning these same matters show that the relation still exists. The difference lies in that man has freedom in the New Testament era; he is no longer bound by law. The Old Testament is more totalitarian in its approach and the New Testament more radical, touching the root of the matter. The basic teaching of both on this matter is the same, but the New Testament has no compilation of specific prescriptions because of the different approach.

This organic involvement is true not only of man collectively but also of man individually. God operates through the individual's personality type, his problems, his religious type, and even his physical abilities and handicaps. [13] In short, there is no antithesis of nature and grace, nor are they mutually exclusive spheres.

Man reacts organically to everything he encounters. A disease affects not only his body but his mental processes and even his spiritual life. The story of Job is not exceptional in this respect. So too, certain factors in man's personality influence his appreciation of related elements of the gospel. His personal socio-phychological problems can block his embracement of certain religious truths or his acceptance of God's will in some particular area of his life. To say that temporal conditions can block the effects of divine grace is not too strong an expression, although it must not be taken in the Pelagian sense. After the rich young ruler refused the offer of salvation when Jesus told him he had to leave all and follow him, Jesus turned to his disciples and said, "how hard it will be for those who have riches to enter the kingdom of God." [14] When the disciples were amazed at his words, Jesus told them just how hard it is: it is impossible. It is as impossible as a camel's passing through the eye of a needle. That is, "with men it is impossible, but not with God: for all things are possible with God." This is truly an impossible possibility. The emphasis upon the divine possibility must not be allowed to blot out the recognition of its human impossibility. Here Jesus teaches that one's economic status affects and is interwoven with his spiritual reactions. And except for the efficacy of divine grace it could constitute an absolute block. Jesus teaches that there is a relation between these two, but he does not say that it is a strictly causal one. One's economic status affects but does not effect his spiritual reactions. [15]

---

[12] Is. 8 : 21.
[13] Cf. Waterink, *Ambtelijke Vakken*, pp. 145, 146.
[14] Mark. 10 : 23.
[15] Cf. also I Tim. 6 : 10, 17.

Everywhere, the Bible tells the same story. Peter admonishes husbands to be considerate of their wives and to honor them in order that their prayers may not be hindered. [16] A disturbed marital relationship in which the husband becomes the master and the wife merely the servant hinders that vital expression of the renewed relation to God. Paul in I Corinthians 7 : 5 assumes a relationship between sexual abstinence and the prayer life, though he does not make it explicit: "Do not refuse one another except perhaps by agreement for a season, that you may devote yourselves to prayer." The Son of Man found the Tempter beside him when he was hungry in the wilderness, and the author of Proverbs 30 prayed to God, "give me neither poverty nor riches; feed me with the food that is needful for me, lest I be full, and deny thee, and say, 'who is the Lord?' or lest I be poor, and steal, and profane the name of my God." [17] Many of the agricultural parables of Jesus either assume or explicitly teach this same truth of man's organic reaction. It is unmistakably clear in Jesus' own exegesis of the parable of the sower. [18] The seed sown on rocky ground is, in modern terminology, the unstable personality who has little order in his psychic life and has not yet found a balance between extremes of reactions and attitudes. He is the eternal adolescent and he is this way spiritually also. He immediately accepts the new teaching, but it is a superficial acceptance that is not anchored in the core of his personality and when tribulation or persecution arises, he again immediately falls away. The seed sown among thorns is the man whose anxiety about this world and whose delight in riches utterly choke out the Word so that it bears no fruit. This passage does not say that one's personality is absolutely determinative of his reaction to the gospel or that only a healthy and well-developed personality can become a Christian. But it does say that these psychic factors affect one's religious response. This is evident also in Paul's exhortation to Timothy, "Flee also youthful lusts." [19] There are irreligious desires which are peculiar to the age of youth with its specific psychosomatic stage of development. These impel a youth to certain religious responses peculiar to his age.

These factors affect man's spiritual response not only negatively as blocks and hindrances but also positively, although not as a material cause. That the personal, self-conscious acceptance of the gospel, usually called "conversion," often coincides with adolescence is no "accidental synchronism of unrelated events." [20] As Waterink has shown in *Puberteit,* four developments occur in the beginning years of puberty:

---

[16]   I Peter 3 : 7.
[17]   Vs. 8, 9.
[18]   Matt. 13 : 18—23.
[19]   II Tim. 2 : 22.
[20]   G. Stanley Hall, *Adolescence,* New York, D. Appleton, 1928, Vol. 2, p. 292. Hall substantiates this temporal correspondence between conversion and adolescence in the pp. 288—292.

the awakening of the consciousness of one's own person, the growing consciousness of the value and worth of things, the growing internal need of ordering one's psychic life, and the seeking of a balance between extremes of reactions and attitudes. [21] These developments in puberty are prerequisites of the religious development of conversion. A child, who is still living in a concrete world and is psychically unable to conceive of abstractions, to distinguish values, and to be aware of his own person is simply unable to come to this kind of self-conscious personal acceptance of the gospel. This is not to say, however, that the person before puberty is not conscious of any relationship to God, but that he is unable to have that type of consciousness which occurs in the religious development called conversion. Reformed churches make the assumption of the necessity of this psychic development when they implicitly limit the public confession of faith to those past the age of puberty. The assumption is that the faith which a child has before this development is different, immature, because psychically he is still a child. But not only are these developments prerequisites of the personal, self-conscious decision, they are also contributing factors in a formal, though not in a material sense. They do not cause the religious decision nor give content to it, but they impel toward *a* decision by creating a sense of unrest and dissatisfaction with the present psychic situation, which stimulates the search for psychic unity and balance in terms of a self-consciously chosen religious position. Thus deep down their search is a search for a god. [22]

The same general situation of a positive influence of these factors is found in the Biblical doctrine of the Covenant. God promises to save through generations. The social unit of the family is utilized in the realization of God's saving will. Although God is not restricted to this method—missionary activity is a real possibility—he says "the promise is unto you, and to your children, and to all that are afar off, even as many as the Lord our God shall call." [23] God saves from father to son by the transmission of his Word from generation to generation. This is no mechanical, automatic process based upon the biological relationship of parent and child but occurs through parental influence and teaching. Therefore, the servants of Abraham [24] and the whole household of the Philippian jailor [25] were given the sign of the covenant. For this reason God requires of parents that they bring up a child in the way he should go, and the liturgical form for infant baptism

---

[21] Wageningen, Gebr. Zomer en Keuning, 1941, pp. 45, 46.

[22] Waterink, *Puberteit*, Wageningen, Gebr. Zomer en Keuning, 1955, p. 133. See chapter ten, "De Ontwikkeling van het Godsdienstig Leven in de Puberteit," pp. 160—181, for a more detailed description of this and other religious developments in puberty.

[23] Acts 2 : 39.

[24] Gen. 17 : 12 explicitly includes the male child who was "bought with money of any stranger, which is not of thy seed."

[25] Acts 16 : 33.

requires assent to the teachings of Holy Scripture and the promise to teach these unto the child, before the sign and seal of the covenant is given. But even faithful observance of these commands gives no absolute guarantee of the child's believing response when he approaches maturity. These social influences are not in the last analysis determinative of the child's response, for some branches of this family tree die and bear no fruit, and then they are cut off and burned. [26] Christ is the pulsating power, the divine cause of the new life, but this new life comes through the branches, from generation to generation. The social structure and influences of the family are involved in a positive way in the realization of God's covenant promise, but are not the final and ultimate cause.

The recognition of the involvement of earthly conditions and processes is not a naturalistic position. To be scientific does not mean that one is less religious. "It is not less religious, but more so, to pour water on an outbreak of fire" than to sit still and "pray to God that it may do no harm." [27] Gerhardus Vos makes an unnecessary and unwarranted limitation of the meaning of those figures of speech taken from the vegetable realm when he says "the point in these is not the naturalness of the development; it is *only the gradualness* [italics mine — M. H.], and gradualness and supernaturalness are not mutually exclusive." [28] Indeed, the point is not the naturalness of the development, and any naturalistic interpretation of the Kingdom must be rejected. Vos is correct in saying also that "gradualness and supernaturalness are not mutually exclusive," but when he limits the point of these figures of speech and parables to gradualness in order to show the error of naturalism, he does not do justice to Jesus' interpretation of the parable of the sower, which teaches that man reacts organically, or Paul's "I planted, Apollos watered" and "we are co-laborers with God," which teach that God works organically in employing human service. The recognition of these two aspects of God's saving activity is not naturalistic; it is the only Biblical way of accounting for the gradualness that Vos himself recognizes in these parables. The involvement of human agents and temporal processes is consistent with Biblical supernaturalism. The Bible does not teach nor, as Berkouwer says, did the Reformers say that it taught, a monergism: "een *alleenwerkzaamheid* Gods, waarin alle mènselijke activiteit wegstuift als kaf voor de wind . . . ." [29] Their rejection of all synergism with its idea of supplementation, does not deny the reality of human activity nor that "er een relatie tussen het Goddelijk en het menselijk werken [is]." [30]

---

[26]   Rom. 11 : 19–21.

[27]   L. D. Weatherhead, *Mystery of Sex*, London, S. C. M. Press, 1945, revised edition, p. 9.

[28]   *Biblical Theology of the Old and New Testaments*, Grand Rapids, W. B. Eerdmans, 1948, pp. 410, 411.

[29]   G. C. Berkouwer, *De Verkiezing Gods*, Kampen, J. H. Kok, 1955, p. 46.

[30]   *Ibid.*, p. 48.

This concept of the positive influence of psychic and social factors upon the spiritual life of man is distinctly different from the naturalistic position of William James, G. Stanley Hall, and Edwin Starbuck, and others of the American school of religious psychology. They attempted to explain all religious experience, including genuine conversion and Christian faith, as the result of natural laws of cause and effect. According to James, religion, psychologically analyzed, posits a wrong part in man and a higher part which is *"conterminous and continuous with a more of the same quality, which is operative in the universe outside him...."* [31] Conversion is the personal identification with the higher part. [32] Thus although James called himself a supernaturalist, [33] his piecemeal supernaturalism is based upon identification of one part of man with this higher reality. Conversion is not a result of an outside influence working through the higher part of man but the victory of one part of man over the other. By accomplishing this man saves *"himself when all his lower being has gone to pieces in the wreck."* [34] Thus all religious experience is man reacting to himself, and each man actually builds his own religion in the way that is most congruous with his personal susceptibilities. [35] Man's religious reaction to the gospel can then be explained as the effects of immanent, natural causes. Starbuck, a pupil of James, is even more explicit: "We proceed on the assumption that this is a lawful universe; that there is no fraction of any part of it which is not entirely determined and conditioned by orderly sequence" and that these laws are ascertainable. [36] "We go one step further, and affirm that there is no event in the spiritual life which does not occur in accordance with *immutable* [italics mine — M. H.] laws." [37] The universe is a closed system for Starbuck and everything that occurs in it is purely the result of natural, temporal causes. Hall shows this same naturalism in his discussion of conversion. "In its most fundamental sense, conversion is a natural, normal, universal, and necessary process at the stage which life pivots over from an autocentric to an heterocentric basis." [38] This school of religious psychology sees psychic and somatic changes not simply as organically interwoven with religious phenomena but as directly causal of them, a true naturalistic position.

This position is the result of that 19th century conception of the universe as a closed system, which Abraham Kuyper so ardently opposed.

---

[31]   *The Varieties of Religious Experience*, New York, Random House, n. d., Modern Library edition, pp. 498, 499.
[32]   *Ibid.*, p. 498.
[33]   *Ibid.*, p. 510.
[34]   *Ibid.*, p. 498.
[35]   *Ibid.*, p. 504.
[36]   *The Psychology of Religion*, London, Walter Scott, 1901, p. 2.
[37]   *Ibid.*, p. 3.
[38]   *Op. cit.*, p. 301. See also p. 303.

The Reformed concept of the organic working of God in his ministries maintains the supernatural cause. Man's assent to the total gospel and the consequent Christian life is not simply a product of the human spirit. Faith is not reducible to physical, psychic, or social causes, but is the reflection of God's salvation in the human heart. Conversion is not a "normal, universal, and necessary process" which is the automatic result of psychosomatic development, but a divinely produced turning to God, which often occurs in and through this psychosomatic development.

Yet, no less ardent was Kuyper's opposition to that view of supernaturalism that conceived of nature with its powers and laws as having a certain independence next to, under, and against God, with which it could resist God's will, but which he could overcome when it suited him. Kuyper called this not a pious but a Godless conception, that consumes supernaturalism. [39] He would place no limits on the activity of God and protested against any concept that viewed nature as something existing or operating in and of itself with God hovering outside, occasionally reaching down to give it direction by introducing a new and different cause, one of a supernatural origin. [40] The manna raining down in the wilderness is from God's power in no greater measure than the grain that grows out of the earth. All things are from God and are his servants. [41] Although this position of Kuyper has been interpreted as naturalism, it is essentially different in that it rejects the view of the universe as a closed system and maintains God's transcendence and the reality of his activity in the world. What Kuyper was seeking to overcome was a less-than-Biblical, fragmatized supernaturalism, a refined form of Deism, and, at the same time, a scientific naturalism which made these earthly factors in and of themselves determinative, a form of Pantheism.

Kuyper's position is not that of the statement of the Jerusalem Meeting of the International Missionary Council: "The one inclusive purpose of the missionary enterprise is to present Jesus Christ to men and women the world over as their Redeemer, and to win them for entrance into the joy of His discipleship. In this endeavour we realize that man is a unity, and that his spiritual life is indivisibly rooted in all his conditions—physical, mental, and social." [42] Man's spiritual life is not "rooted in" these conditions. It is involved in them, but it does not find its source of power, its life, its food, its nature in these conditions. One cannot Christianize peoples by Christianizing their civilization, as the International Missionary Council seems to assume when it speaks of education

---

[39]   E Voto Dordraceno, Amsterdam, J. A.Wormser, 1892, Vol. 1, p. 238.
[40]   Ibid., p. 239.
[41]   Ibid., p. 240.
[42]   The Christian Mission in Relation to Rural Problems, London, Oxford University Press, 1928, Vol. 6 of the report of the Jerusalem meeting of the I.M.C., p. 287.

as the "fundamental method" and of redeeming communities by working at the major economic and social problems of those communities. [43]

This is not the Reformed concept of God's organic activity, as advanced by Kuyper. Faith is not reducible. The Freudian school of psychology is wrong when it reduces faith to biological or psychic processes, the American school of religious psychology when it reduces faith to psychosomatic processes, and the report of the International Missionary Council when it apparently reduces faith to physical, mental, and social processes. Yet these processes are organically involved in God's saving activity.

A consistently theistic creationism demands the recognition of this truth. God did not create the universe, give it order and laws, activate it, and then withdraw when time and history began except, perhaps, for a few irruptive moments in which he produced miracles. This is a deistic creationism. Theistic creationism, on the other hand, maintains God's creative activity in the temporal processes of the universe. A second phase of God's creation began after the *creatio ex nihilo*, which was not purely "irruptive" or "ictic" but also "processional." [44] More precisely, "the irruptive and the processive are not two separate relationships: rather are they, like the warp and woof of a single fabric, two dimensions of the single relationship of Creator and creature." [45] God is active as a transcendent force and as an immanent force at the same time in accomplishing his ends. The most clearly irruptive acts of God, such as revelation and the incarnation, have a processional dimension and utilize human agents with their creatural potentials. In producing the Holy Scriptures God resorted to an impulsive Peter, a reflective John, and a philosophical Paul, and the "incarnation was not achieved without recourse to creature and creaturely potential." [46] The evaluation of this position as less religious or less Christian betrays a deistic bias and implicitly denies God's immanence in an attempt to preserve his transcendence. But these two are not alternatives nor are they alternating relationships, each taking its turn in history. A truly theistic creationism maintains both as "two different aspects of a single relationship." [47] This processional, immanent dimension of God's activity means that creatures and creatural potentials, conditions, and processes are involved in the realization of salvation, and thus it necessitates a consideration of the psychic and social aspects of the individual in the church's ministry to the individual.

[43] *Ibid.*, pp. 298, 299.

[44] The terminology employed here and the subsequent development of theistic creationism is derived from an excellent, Reformed statement of the relation between divine activity and natural procession by Leonard Verduin, "Toward a Theistic Creationism," *The Reformed Journal*, Vol. 6 (October, 1956), pp. 6–9; Vol. 6 (November, 1956), pp. 9–13.

[45] *Ibid.*, part one, p. 9.

[46] *Ibid.*, part two, p. 10.

[47] *Ibid.*, part one, p. 9.

This necessity is accented by the comprehensiveness of this salvation of God. A study comittee of the Nederlandse Zendingsraad on the Biblical foundations of missions, composed of J. H. Bavinck, H. J. Ridderbos, and others, closely considered this aspect of salvation in relation to the comprehensive approach of missions. They concluded that neither in the Old Testament nor in the New does the word "salvation" have an *exclusively spiritual* meaning but comprises the *whole life of man*. Salvation is the restoration of life as fruit of the restoration of communion with God through reconciliation and forgiveness. [48]

This comprehensive salvation is expressed in the Old Testament by the word *shalom*. The central importance of this concept in the Old Testament is pointed out by Hastings: "Among the blessings to which Israel looks forward in the Messianic time none is more emphasized than peace." [49] This word, *shalom*, is a common, everyday word with a wide variety of usages, yet often in the Old Testament it is filled with a concrete religious meaning. [50] The word "peace" is not a sufficiently comprehensive translation, for the basic meaning is welfare, with a very strong and clear preponderance toward the material side. [51] Therefore it can refer to physical health, as in Jeremiah 6 : 14, or prosperity with its resulting contentment, as in Genesis 26 : 29. Caspari says that a development in the meaning of the term can be traced in the Old Testament from the original sense of material welfare, of which God was recognized as the source, to a later, more comprehensive meaning of salvation, which is a religious term that embraces all the blessings Israel expects from God, both in the present time and in the age of the Messiah: [52] national peace, freedom from want, freedom from oppression, a renewed harmony in nature, etc. This new comprehensive meaning comes to clear expression in Psalm 85 : 9—13: "Surely his salvation (*shalom*) is nigh them that fear him ; that glory may dwell in our land." Then in the following verses this *shalom* is described: "Mercy and truth are met together; righteousness and peace have kissed each other. Truth shall spring out of the earth; and righteousness shall look down from heaven. Yea, the Lord shall give that which is good; and our land shall yield her increase. Righteousness shall go before him and shall set us in the way of his steps." The covenant of

---

[48] "Rapport uitgebracht aan de *Nederlandse Zendingsraad* door de studiecommissie inzake '*De Bijbelse grondslagen van de zending.*'" *De Heerbaan*, August, 1951, p. 211.

[49] J. Hastings (ed.), *Dictionary of the Bible*, Edinburgh, T. and T. Clark, 1900, Vol. 3, p. 733.

[50] Gerhard Kittel (ed.), *Theologisches Wörterbuch zum Neuen Testament*, Stuttgart, W. Kohlhammer, 1933–, Vol. 2, p. 400.

[51] *Ibid.*

[52] L. W. Caspari, *Vorstellung und Wort "Friede" in Alten Testament*, Gütersloh, C. Bertelsmann, 1910, p. 161. Caspari summarizes this development in Ch. 12, pp. 128–162.

salvation then receives the name "the covenant of peace" [53] and the coming Messiah is called the "Prince of Peace." [54]

The Old Testament concepts of righteousness and justice also show this comprehensiveness of salvation. They are not to be understood only in the juridical sense. Righteousness is always a constituent element of God's salvation and includes social, ethical, social-economic, and political restoration. [55] The idea of reformation in these areas of life is essential to the concept righteousness. [56] In the prophetic books "there is a marked tendency for Righteousness to have special reference to the needs of the poor, the widow, and the orphan." [57] Righteousness is more than a merely ethical word. In the prophetic books it has invaded the salvation vocabulary. It is actually "incidental that *tsedeq* stands for justice. It is incidental because *tsedeq* stands for the establishment of God's will in the land, and secondarily for justice, because that in part is God's will. It is 'in part,' because God's will is wider than justice." [58] In many instances [59] it means a benevolence going beyond strict justice. [60] The concept of holiness also has this comprehensive significance. It came to "include righteousness as the main element of its content," [61] and therefore any definition which limits it to the ideas of purity, morality, and ethical rectitude must be rejected, for it "has thus stopped short of expressing that wider activity of God on behalf of the helpless ones . . . ." [62]

Though the comprehensiveness of salvation is less explicit in the New Testament, there is no essential difference. The paraenetical sections of Paul's letters and the Biblical books by other apostles are concerned with the believer's attitudes and actions in marriage, family, social, and political life. [63] No clearcut distinction is made between these sections and those specifically concerned with the proclamation of Christ. Notice how Paul in the letter to the Romans, chapters five through fourteen, speaks of justification by faith, election, the unity of the church, social relations, family relations, the citizen's relation to his government, and the use of meat, without any noticeable sign that he was aware of a significant transition of subject matter. The reformation of these areas of life were all part of salvation for Paul.

The church therefore has not only the right but the duty to concern

---

[53] Is. 54 : 10, Ezek. 34 : 25, 37 : 26, and others.
[54] Is. 9 : 6.
[55] Cf. Lev. 19 and Deut. 19 ff.
[56] Cf. "Rapport," *De Heerbaan*, p. 211.
[57] Norman H. Snaith, *The Distinctive Ideas of the Old Testament,* London, Epworth Press, 1944, p. 79.
[58] *Ibid.,* p. 70.
[59] Ezek. 18 : 19, 21; Ps. 33 : 5; and many others.
[60] Snaith, *op. cit.,* p. 71.
[61] *Ibid.,* p. 79.
[62] *Ibid.*
[63] Cf. e.g. Col. 3 and Eph. 6.

herself with the penetration of the gospel in the whole life of man. [64]
The ground of this comprehensiveness of salvation may be called the
emphatic religious realism of the Bible: God and world do not stand
over against each other, except through the sin of man, and then never
dualistically, according to their original essence. [65] Salvation is not a
withdrawal from this world but the restoration of its original
harmony.

Jesus, too, sent out his disciples to preach the gospel and to heal the
sick. Paul in Romans 15 : 18, 19 defines his missionary task as the
winning of obedience by word and deed. These deeds are not of a
completely other order from the medical work, social work, and economic work of today. They are both an expression of God's grace unto
a rebellious world and a result of God's saving activity here on earth,
overcoming the effects of sin, [66] however much they may differ in other
respects.

God's organic activity in saving man, man's organic reaction, and the
comprehensiveness of the salvation revealed in Scripture require that
poimenics, as one of the theological sciences of God's ministry through
his church, include sociological and psychological studies as constituent
elements. Without these it is an incomplete science. The scope of the
church's ministry to the individual is much more extensive than only
that of the direct ministry of proclamation. This ministry is accomplished
not only through kerygma but also through diakonia and koinonia. All
three are indivisibly a part of the messianic shalom. Hoekendijk
describes the interrelation of these three in his explication of another
ministry of the church, the ministry of evangelism.

> The kerygma is the proclamation that the shalom has come . . . .
> But, with the kerygma alone, in isolation, the evangelist soon be-
> comes a more or less interesting orator. He needs the manifestation
> of the koininia of which he is a part and he has to justify himself
> as a witness of the Messiah-Servant in his diakonia.
> The koinonia manifests the shalom, as it is present among men.
> But we need the continuous reminder of the kerygma, the inter-
> pretation of this shalom as the salvation of the Messiah, and the
> diakonia should prevent this shalom being used in a self-sufficient
> way.
> The diakonia translates the shalom into the language of humble

[64] "Rapport," De Heerbaan, p. 212.
[65] Ibid., p. 211.
[66] Cf. Eduard Thurneysen, Die Lehre von der Seelsorge, Zollikon-Zürich,
Evangelischer Verlage A.-G., 1957, p. 198. "Aber wichtig ist, dass für den Seelsorger
das Faktum einer Heilung erst dann wirklich erfüllt ist, wenn der Patient seine
Genesung als ihm von der Hand Gottes geschenkte Gabe verstehen und dafür
danken kann. Diese Gabe ist in jedem Falle die Gabe der Vergebung, der
Gnade. . . ." Cf. also the section "Heilung als Vergebung," pp. 208–214.

service. But if we isolate this *diakonia* or give it an undue emphasis, then the evangelist soon becomes a sentimental philanthropist. He must never forget that he cannot render real service if he deprives man of the *kerygma* and leaves him outside the *koinonia*. [67]

Hoekendijk might justifiably have added that all three are not only witnesses to the messianic *shalom* but are part of that *shalom* itself. Salvation is reception and impartation of the good news of *kerygma*, the reception and giving of *diakonia*, and the reception and giving of *koinonia*. When a believer gives these, he conveys *shalom*.

Many books written on the church's ministry to the individual limit this ministry too narrowly to the sphere of personal proclamation of the Word. Thurneysen, for example, says "Seelsorge findet sich in der Kirche vor als Ausrichtung des Wortes Gottes an den Einzelnen." [68] His further development of the nature of "Seelsorge" in the following three hundred pages shows that he is consciously limiting "Seelsorge" to the "Ausrichtung des Wortes Gottes." That may indeed be the kernel of the church's ministry to the individual, but its area is much more extensive. The investigation of the social and psychic aspects of man and his problems is a legitimate and even essential part of the theological science of poimenics. Such a consideration is not an implicit capitulation to naturalism, for it does not deny God's activity in man's religious response but rather affirms God's activity also in these other aspects of life.

The church's ministry to the individual must also care for the circumstances in which the man lives in part because they are involved in his receptivity to the gospel. They do not finally determine his reaction either positively or negatively, but they do have an organic influence. One can call this the indirect ministry of the church to distinguish it from the direct ministry described by Thurneysen, but it is nevertheless ministry of the church. It is not always necessary that the church do this indirect ministry as institute, through her office bearers. But it is necessary that the church as the body of believers do this ministry. In many cases efficiency will demand the organization of groups or bureaus for one particular aspect of that ministry.

But the church must care for the circumstances and conditions of men also because she loves the whole man. She desires his material welfare as well as his spiritual growth. The church as the body of believers feels no inconsistency in attempting to remedy injustice, in promoting psychic and physical health, and in giving guidance to men

---

[67] J. C. Hoekendijk, "The Call to Evangelism," *The International Review of Missions*, April, 1950, pp. 171, 172. Even though I cannot agree with every point made in this quotation, Hoekendijk's thesis of the interrelation of these three elements in the ministry of the church is valid.

[68] *Op. cit.*, p. 9.

with personal problems. This is part of her task as the bearer of *shalom.*

Therefore, the church's ministry to a specific group will require, first, the formation of a sociological and psychological picture of the life of this group and especially of the difficulties with which they wrestle and which can or do hinder the development of the joyful life of faith. This picture is an integral part of the theological science of specialized poimenics because it is necessary for the understanding of how God works in this specific group and how they react to the gospel. The psychological and sociological givens of a group have an importance far beyond the determination of correct technique or method. [69]

Secondly, the church will have to consider the question whether and in how far it is possible to change those psychic and social impediments, whether through the direct intervention of the organization of the church or through the employment of other agencies.

Finally, the church, considering the particular characteristics and conditions of a certain group, must determine how she can bring the message of the whole gospel in the most efficient manner. The church desires more than just the initial acceptance of Christ as Savior. She also wishes to promote a life of reconciliation to God through faith in Jesus Christ, which is directed according to the revealed will of God and devoted to his service. She is not content with laying the foundation, she wishes also to build a mighty structure upon that foundation. She wishes to edify. Therefore she must feel it her right and her duty to intervene in every psychic or social condition which impedes this spiritual construction.

This thesis, therefore, is chiefly a sociological and psychological study of one homogeneous group within the church. Nevertheless, it is a theological study. The psychic and social characteristics of this group are studied only in so far as they are involved in the spiritual response to the whole revelation of God, in so far as they have a negative influence upon this group's efforts to live according to the revealed will of God and devoted to his service.

Intent of the Thesis

This thesis applies the above-defined concept of the church's ministry to a particular group within the church, the older unmarried. The social problem of the older unmarried, especially the older unmarried woman, [70] is described and analyzed in chapter two. Society's evaluation of this group, the underlying cause of this evaluation and some other factors contributing to it, and the roles this group is expected to play

---

[69] R. Kooistra has made an extensive study of the importance of sociology for theology. See his book, *De Gereformeerde Theoloog en de Sociologie,* Franeker, Wever, 1955, especially Ch. 4, "Het Ambt."

[70] The reason for this limitation will become evident in the following chapter.

in society are examined. An investigation of the personal problems of the older unmarried follows in chapter three. This order was chosen because many of the personal problems are the direct result of society's adverse evaluation or are significantly modified by it. Consequently, these personal problems can neither be understood nor solved apart from an understanding of these social factors. Chapter three considers those problems commonly a result of being unmarried in a Western type of society and those which acquire a particular urgency or a significantly different configuration for the older unmarried. Thus not all problems which the older unmarried can and do have are considered, for this would include nearly all of the problems common to mankind. For example, sorrow over the death of a relative or dear friend is not handled, but loneliness is since this problem has both a particular urgency and a significantly different configuration for the older unmarried. Chapter four contains some conclusions for the science and practice of the church's ministry to this group.

Area of the Thesis

The group studied in this thesis is limited to older single men and women. The terms "unmarried," "single," and "older unmarried" will be used in the restricted sense of "never married" unless otherwise stated. Both widows and widowers and divorced men and women will be excluded because their social and psychic problems are not homogeneous with those of the "never married." For example, the problem of being alone is other for widows or divorcees because their having been married changes the nature of that adjustment they must make. They adjust from living with the husband they once had. Also, that many of them have children from this previous marriage modifies the problem. Another important difference is that this previous marriage affects society's attitude toward them. [71] The forty-year-old widow, the forty-year-old divorcee, and the forty-year-old spinster are given different roles to play. The widow is expected to be sedate, the divorcee *blasé*, and the spinster dehydrated. Even the sexual adjustment of widows and divorcees is altered by their having been married. Their problem is not modified by the social factor of "having missed an experience which society highly values" but is a problem of "what to do with an awakened and once satisfied drive."

The term "older" in "older unmarried" refers to those age thirty and above. This delimitation according to age is also necessary to form a homogeneous group. Those who are still in their late teens or twenties, for example, are not old maids or bachelors in either their

---

[71] See Ch. 2. In this section of the introduction occasional statements, especially those dealing with the problems of the unmarried, will be found which cannot conveniently be substantiated until later, when these subjects are handled in detail. Only the most important of these will be noted.

own or society's estimation. The social problem of the older unmarried [72] does not apply to them. They face little personal adjustment to their unmarried status because they still expect it to change. Usually they are living within a family group and are not self-supporting and self-sufficient. Therefore, they have a different social role and different social and psychic problems.

The choice of thirty as the point of division is somewhat arbitrary. Between the ages of twenty-five and thirty-five the personal problems of the unmarried as well as the social attitude toward them undergoes a change. Although the marriage prospects for this age group are still relatively high, [73] society begins to tag them with the names and roles of "old maid" and "bachelor" somewhere between these age limits. They are the ones who "couldn't find a mate" and their situation is regarded as having a high degree of permanency. They are no longer seen as in the group of "not yet married." Their being unmarried takes on a different significance. Regardless of their statistical prospects for marrying at some later time in life, they and the rest of society consider them outside the group of "yet to marry" unless this prospect is immediately present, and they must adjust to the personal problems of the unmarried state.

Secondly, it is usually between the ages of twenty-five and thirty-five that the personal problems inherent to their unmarried status arise or receive a new cast. [74] Sometime between these ages the unmarried man or woman begins to realize the probability of his or her never marrying and the necessity of an adjustment to this state and its problems. All these changes are gradual and the realization of the consequences will be earlier in one individual than in another. Seldom, however, does it begin in America before the age of twenty-five—except in those areas where women are expected to marry very young—or after the age of thirty-five. Therefore, thirty was chosen [75] as a mean, not as an absolute boundary. In applying the conclusions of this thesis to any specific group of older unmarried the marriage-age mores and individual differences must be taken into account.

---

[72] See Ch. 2. for support of this and other statements about the social position of the older unmarried.

[73] Of the 30-year-old single men 72 per cent will still marry at some time in their lives and 55 per cent of the 30-year-old single women. By the age of 35 the marrying ratio is still one of every two men and one of every three single women. Harry Hansen (ed.), *The World Almanac and Book of Facts for 1958*, New York, The New York World-Telegram, 1958, p. 313.

[74] See Ch. 3.

[75] Other studies which have also chosen thirty as the lower age boundary of this group are A. J. Bladergroen, "De Werkende Vrouw Boven 30 Jaar," *Mens en Onderneming*, Vol. 7, 1953, p. 360; Kimball Young, *Personality and Problems of Adjustment*, New York, F. S. Crafts, 1940, p. 572; and D. J. Deegan *The Stereotype of the Single Woman in American Novels*, New York, King's Crown Press, 1951, p. x.

Hereafter, the terms "single" and "unmarried" will be used as synonomous with "older unmarried," designating that group over thirty years who have never married. The common terms "bachelor," "old maid," and "spinster" will be avoided because of the emotional connotations attached to them. [76] The term "marriage" and its derivatives, unless specifically stated to the contrary, will be used in the broad sense, including all those elements which are usually associated with marriage or are considered a result of it—as, for example, the married partners living together, sexual intercourse, procreation, and a reasonably harmonious family life. [77]

The third delimitation of the thesis subject is geographical and cultural. The question of both the existence and the nature of the social problem of the unmarried is determined by the type of society in which they live. For example, the standard of living, the level of employment, and the social mores are major factors in determining whether unmarried women live alone and if so, whether they have only rooms or a private apartment or home. This in turn affects the personal problems of loneliness, intimate contact with other age groups, and their adjustment to old age. Therefore it was necessary to limit the thesis subject to one country, the United States. However, since America has an historical continuity with Western European cultures, much of the analysis and many of the conclusions will be applicable to the older unmarried of other lands. But the differences of subsequent historical development of social attitudes, economic position, mores, etc. are sufficiently great to demand a separate treatment.

Importance of the Problem

Eight percent of the men and seven percent of the women in the United States over the age of thirty are unmarried. [78] In 1956 this group of older unmarried totaled 6,929,000, of which 3,748,000 were men and 3,181,000 were women. [79] If these figures are compared with the total male and female population thirty years and over, [80] one out of every twelve men and one out of every fourteen women of this age are single.

Although this group of single men is larger than the group of women, the marriage possibilities for the men are greater. In computing the

---

[76]   These connotations and their implications will be considered in Ch. 2.

[77]   This may give the impression that marriage has only advantages and singleness, only disadvantages and problems. This conclusion should not be drawn, for the purpose of the references to the married state is not a comparison of the numbers or importance of the problems of each state but an explanation of those problems and adjustments which the older unmarried must face because they are single.

[78]   U. S. Bureau of the Census, *Statistical Abstract of the United States 1957*, p. 45.

[79]   Hansen, *op. cit.*, p. 263.

[80]   *Ibid.*, p. 262.

statistical possibilities of marriage the number of divorced men and
women, widows, and widowers over the age of thirty must be included.
In this total group there is an excess of 5,198,000 marriageable women.
But since the average age when marrying in the United States is twenty
for women and twenty-three for men, [81] relatively few marriages occur
after the age of thirty. Therefore the percentage of males and females
who are still single remains nearly constant. For any age group over
thirty, eight percent of the men and seven percent of the women are
still single. [82]

The poimenical study of this group, the older unmarried, is necessary,
therefore, because it is a group that has a social problem (chapter two),
that has homogeneous personal problems (chapter three), and that is
a significantly large proportion of the American population.

---

[81]   U. S. Bureau of the Census, *op. cit.*, p. 72.
[82]   *Ibid.*, p. 45.

CHAPTER II

THE SOCIAL PROBLEM OF THE OLDER UNMARRIED

Introduction

This chapter is not a sociological summary of the actual place and role of the older unmarried in American society. It is rather a study of what society thinks of the older unmarried, how society expects them to act, and how society judges them. Of interest here is not what kind of persons the other unmarried actually are and what role they actually play in society. Although these two elements, social expectations and the actual social role, are reciprocally influential, they do not necessarily coincide and can, therefore, be separated. Both shape the single person's personal problems. Both affect his efforts to live the full Christian life, directed according to God's revealed will and devoted to his service.

Sociological study of the older unmarried has made evident that the social attitudes and expectations are more uniform than the actual social role of the unmarried. These attitudes and expectations have an adverse effect upon nearly every personal problem of the unmarried and thus need particular attention. The specifics of the unmarried's actual role in society, however, are so diverse and have such multiform effects that they can better be handled in direct connection with the personal problems to which they are related. Therefore, these specifics will be treated in chapter three. But since so few sociological studies of the actual social role of the older unmarried have been made, only a few of its influences can be indicated.

Before describing the social problem of the unmarried, it is necessary to consider the question, what is a social problem? What makes any specific group a social problem? What is the common factor in Negroes, juvenile delinquents, criminals, and the older unmarried that makes all of them social problems?

Both the Negro and the juvenile delinquent are American social problems. But the latter is a social problem because he harms society and the former because society discriminates against him. Yet they have a common element: they do not measure up to the standards and ideals of that society in which they live. To the degree in which society's norms of measurement are real and significant, to that same degree the deviation of any group is socially condemned.

These standards and ideals have many forms. They may be mental images in the social consciousness such as the image of the ideal mother, of the successful businessman, or of the perfect husband. They may be legally formulated moral standards, making anyone who deviates a criminal as well as a social problem. But if the legally formulated standard does not coincide with society's real standard, if society actually approves the illegal action, the deviating group is criminal but is not a social problem. Not the formulation but the social attitude determines whether any group is a problem. Prohibition in the 1920's is an example of disconcurrence between the real and the legal standards of society. Or, these standards may be economic. The poor are a social problem only if poverty is a deviation from society's idea. If the vow of poverty is consistent with the ideals of a community (as for example, the beggar monks of the Middle Ages or the holy men of India), those who have taken this vow are no social problem; but those who are poor for a reason other than the vow of poverty are. Society's ideals may also be racial. If being Caucasian is one of society's ideals, the Negro is a social problem.

Being unmarried, too, becomes a social problem only if there has been a prior judgment that this is a socially undesirable status, that is, only if this status does not conform in some way to the standards and ideals of the society. The seriousness of the social problem of the unmarried depends upon the seriousness of society's judgment of the deviation from its ideal. Society's evaluation of the unmarried state is determined by the measure in which that state serves the economic, political, biological, cultural, and religious purposes which man has been assigned in that society.

At heart, all these purposes assigned to man are religious value-judgments. For example, in the Middle Ages sexual continence was considered to be one of the highest virtues, and taking the ecclesiastical vow of celibacy was socially honored. Remaining unmarried because of a religious vow of celibacy harmonized with the standards and ideals of society in the Middle Ages, and those who took this vow were no social problem. The same situation is found today in many Catholic countries and in Oriental societies. But, if, as in some primitive societies, the propagation of the race is one of the essential purposes and duties of man, and if a man's value is measured chiefly by the number of children he fathers, and if parenthood is socially approved only within the marriage relationship, then singleness is socially condemned, and social pressures are brought to bear to make the individual conform.

Such social attitudes and pressures were discovered by Margaret Mead in the village of Bajoeng Gedé on the island of Bali. On Bali the unmarried man is denied full social status; he is forever associated with the young boys and remains at the foot of the social ladder because he is not a father. "Marriage is . . . socially enforced, a way of producing children whom one must have to be socially complete." [1]

---

[1]   *Male and Female*, London, Victor Gollancz, 1949, p. 227.

Many Oriental peoples make a similar social judgment of singleness because they believe that sons and/or daughters are necessary in order to provide post-burial service for the parents. Since this service affects the deads' position in the next world, parenthood is a very important social ideal. Failure to marry—and thus to become parents—is deemed a serious loss of face.

Both of these examples show that social attitudes are determined by social standards and ideals. These standards and ideals rest ultimately upon religious presuppositions about the nature of man, his purpose, and his duty.

Thus, a group which is a social problem in one society is not in another because the standards and ideals of the two societies differ. Whether a group is a social problem must be determined by a study of the social attitudes toward the group, society's evaluation of them, and society's expectations with regard to their behavior, their contribution to society, and their response to society. After the social problem has been recognized, a choice must be made between two possible solutions: a group can be made socially acceptable either by overcoming the factors causing the deviation or by changing society's standards and ideals. The social therapy of criminals, for example, generally follows the first course and sociologists dealing with racial discrimination the second. The second course, the changing of society's standards and ideals, is neither an impossible nor an illegitimate task of social therapy since these standards and ideals are socially conditioned. [2]

Therefore, this chapter includes a study of American social attitudes toward the older unmarried, the standard by which this evaluation is made, and the direction in which the solution must be sought.

Any sociologist or anthropologist has one important difficulty in studying a highly complex civilization, a difficulty which is aggravated when the society is a melting pot of cultures, as is American society. There are no uniform and simple social expectations and attitudes common to all individuals because there is no universally accepted standard of the value and purpose of man. [3] Therefore the difficulty: it is impossible to give a universally valid summary of the social evaluation of the older unmarried or a complete analysis of all the factors influencing the standards by which this evaluation is made. However, even a complex society such as that of America has common elements. The attitudes reflected in and dispersed through the various media of communication, through literature, through folklore, humor, and linguistic connotations of terms used to designate a group, can be taken as a valid representation of the attitudes of American society as a whole,

---

[2] For example, a society's environment always influences its ideology. Cf. V. Klein, *The Feminine Character*, London, Kegan Paul, 1946, pp. 113—115.

[3] Mead, *Male and Female*, p. 140, "But in complex modern societies, there are no such clear expectations [as in primitive societies] . . . , even for one class or occupational group or rural region."

although not necessarily of all its parts. Nevertheless, no group totally escapes the influence of these media and, consciously or unconsciously, each person assimilates common social attitudes to some degree. Through a study of American literature, humor, social patterns, and the connotations of linguistic labels, substantiated by the considered conclusions of American sociologists, the social attitudes toward the older unmarried are investigated in this chapter.

Society's Attitudes Toward and Evaluations of the Older Unmarried

Society makes no uniform assessment of the entire older unmarried group. There are different judgments of different parts of this group and, as a result, different attitudes to these various parts. Therefore, some older unmarried constitute a serious social problem, and others do not.

The most important division society makes is the one based on the sex of the older unmarried person. The attitude toward the unmarried man differs significantly from the attitude toward the unmarried woman. The difference between the social attitude toward single man and the attitude toward single woman is already evident in the terms used in designation. About the age of thirty, when most women are already married, the single woman acquires the label "old maid." And at about the same age the single man acquires the label "bachelor." The connotations of these two terms are of very different qualities. The connotations of the term "old maid" are strongly derogatory. It is a term that people avoid in formal conversation, and yet it is probably the one most commonly used. Literally it means an aged, though immature member of the female sex. Its connotation is very close to this literal meaning: the "old maid" is female, but not quite a complete woman. Once a woman has, in the judgment of society, left the category of "not yet married" and entered the category of "never married," society gives her a different valuation and changes its attitude toward her.

The older single woman is a favorite subject of American humor—together with such figures as the mother-in-law, the farmer's daughter, and the Arkansas hillbilly. Her marital status has become so important socially that it fixes society's judgment of her person. Society classifies her as an "old maid" and through a conditioned reflex to this term, calls up a negative stereotype. This stereotype of the single woman is the cause of social derision and makes her a fit subject for jokes and anecdotes.

The derisive attitude toward the older unmarried woman is so deeply rooted that society can hardly recognize her as a suitable subject for serious discussion. One sociologist who worked with the problem of the single woman reported the chuckling query of a "professor of wide reputation . . . , 'What is it you want to do—write a guidebook for the old maid?'" [4] Another sociologist began a lecture on the single woman with the statement: "When I first said that I wanted to talk about single women some of my friends laughed." [5] The author of this thesis has had similar experiences. The first mention of his thesis subject almost invariably produced a smile and often a veiled deprecation of the subject. Although the single woman is a social problem surrounded by prejudice and taboo, she is not considered a sufficiently dignified subject for acedemic research. At very best, society's attitude to the single woman is one of condescending pity: she is seen as a poor woman who missed one of the most important things of life; as a handicapped person, to be classified with the cripple and the deformed. [6]

The term "bachelor" is generally not derogatory. It has no strong negative connotation. It is chiefly a relational term, one which describes a man's marital status and not one which makes a judgment upon his person. It may have emotional connotations, but they are not strong. And, they are usually favorable: free, dashing, unincumbered, not entangled by responsibilities. The positive connotations of the term "bachelor" are sufficiently wide-spread to support the term "bachelor girl" as a journalistic euphemism for "old maid."

Superficially at least, the bachelor is envied by married men—while the married woman is envied by single women. At stag parties men sing, "I wish I were single again." The bridegroom is described as "hooked" or "caught," as though no man would willingly marry. The disparagingly humorous attitude toward the bridegroom is a marked contrast toward the attitude to the bride. The wedding is seen as a major step forward for her. Much American humor is based on the common social conception that for a man singleness is preferable to marriage. [7] The social attitude toward the bachelor, expressed in American humor, is adequately summarized in the old saying: "A married man is a man with a past, and the bachelor a man with a future." Admittedly, these expressions are only half-serious judgments; but they are that. Marriage is generally considered a liability for a man and a laudatory accomplishment for a woman. Both American humor and the terminology designating the single person show the general social attitude toward the unmarried woman is pity or derision, and the attitude to the unmarried man generally to be envy.

It is noteworthy that the strength of society's negative attitude toward the single woman is considerably greater than the strength of its positive

[4] Dorothy Deegan, *The Stereotype of the Single Woman in American Novels,* New York, King's Crown Press, 1951, p. ix.

[5] Margery Fry, *The Single Woman,* London, Delisle, 1953, p. 1.

[6] Mead, *Male and Female,* p. 323.

[7] Theodor Reikx gives the example of a cartoon which "pictured a small boy with his father at the zoo. The caption gave the dialogue between them. The boy asks: 'Daddy, do asses marry?' The father answers: 'Only asses marry.'" *Of Love and Lust,* New York, Farrar, Straus and Cudahy, 1957, p. 389.

attitude toward the single man. Society's admiration of the single man is only half-serious, but its censure of the single woman is unambiguous and forceful. Society is relatively indifferent toward the marital status of a man, but the marital status of a woman is important. It is important enough to maintain separate titles for the married and the unmarried woman in order to identify immediately the marital status of each. All unmarried members of the female sex, regardless of age, are addressed as "Miss" and all married females as "Mrs." It is also significant that the distinction does not refer simply to the present marital status—that is, whether a woman is now married to a man and living with him. Many divorcees and nearly all widows retain the title of "Mrs." Society wants to know whether a woman has ever, at any time and for any length of time, been married.

By comparison, society cares little about the marital status of a man. Again, two titles are used, "Master" and "Mister"; but the point of distinction is not marital status, as with women, but maturity. When a boy becomes a man, his title changes from "Master" to "Mister," whether he is married or not. Marriage is not socially important for a man. He is rarely described or identified in terms of his marriage. "To a man, marriage belongs to his personal life," writes M. E. Harding. "It has relatively little to do with his position in the community or with his relation to his work. But to a woman the situation is entirely different; marriage is much more far-reaching in its effects. Her whole life is altered by it, her social status is completely changed. There is a world of difference between whether she is a Mrs. or a Miss. As Mrs. So-and-so she is accepted by the world and accorded a deference and attention which she would never receive if she were still a Miss." [8] Margaret Mead agrees that the marital status of a woman is much more important to society than the marital status of a man, since "marriage is regarded virtually as the most honorable full-time job [a woman] can have. . . ." [9]

Both the uniformity of society's evaluation of the single woman and the strength of society's negative attitude are caused by a very rigid and widespread stereotype. The stereotype of the older single woman is so uniform and so commonly accepted that the statement "she is a born old maid" communicates to all people. They have a common mental image of the personality and the behavior of an older unmarried woman.

There is no comparable picture of the unmarried man. It may be seriously questioned whether one can even speak of a stereotype of the single man, since society's mental image of him has little rigidity and uniformity. At most, one can speak of various stereotypes of single men. There is the footloose and fancy-free, man-about-town bachelor,

---

8   *The Way of All Women,* New York, Longmans, Green and Company, 1933, p. 137.

9   "Woman's Social Position," *The Journal of Educational Sociology,* April, 1944, p. 454.

who wines and dines a different blond every night, who is a regular first-nighter, is socially polished, and financially secure. There is also the lonely recluse, who, embittered at the world, withdraws from society. And there is the mild, shrinking, colorless little bachelor who lives with his mother and elderly sisters, is passive to his environment, and lacks all self-determination. There is the strong, husky, outdoor-type bachelor, the man's man, who does a rough job of mending and washing his clothes but is self-sufficient enough not to miss a woman's care. There are many more types, but no one "bachelor type." Society has no ready-made picture of the single man, and therefore has no single emotional reflex toward him. His singleness does not so qualify him that his real person is overshadowed.

However, society makes one other distinction—besides that of the sex of the single person—which determines her attitude toward the older unmarried. She distinguishes between the voluntarily single and the involuntarily single. Society's generally favorable attitude toward the single man is modified in the case of the man who does not marry because he cannot find any women who would have him. His freedom remains enviable, but his involuntary singleness is regarded as a failure for which he is responsible. However, not involuntary singleness but voluntary modifies the attitude toward the single woman. If society is convinced that she has remained unmarried for some reason other than lack of opportunity—if, for example, she has devoted her life to some ideal that excludes the possibility of marriage—the adverse evaluation of her is softened. Her singleness, however, is still seen as a limitation: although she may have the qualities necessary for marriage, she has been deprived of the formative influence of marriage and of all its other benefits.

Since the prevailing social attitude toward the single man is one of approval, he is no social problem. The single woman is a social problem. She has deviated from society's ideal and her deviation is seriously censured. To solve the social problem of the single woman, the source of society's evaluation of her, contained in a stereotype, must be traced, and the premise which forms the foundation for society's evaluation must be judged.

The Source of Society's Stereotype of the Single Woman

A stereotype not only reveals social attitudes, but it is one of the chief means of perpetuating these attitudes. [10] The stage, motion pictures, television, fiction, cartoons, the press, and advertisements use stereotypes as a ready means of characterization. Repeated and general use of the stereotype of the single woman has disseminated and strengthened it in the social mind.

---

[10] Deegan, *op. cit.*, p. xiii.

Yet, the stereotype of the single woman has undergone extensive revisions at various times in American history. Each metamorphosis seems to have occurred when society's concept of the marriageable woman changed. [11] The stereotype of the single woman existed already at the founding of the country. In the heritage of many early American settlers the marriageable woman was expected to be gracious, charming, dependent, and helpless. The unmarried woman was classified as one who failed to meet these requirements, and the image of the "old maid" was that of a masculine, independent, self-sufficient person. But the American frontier demanded another type of wife. Meekness, timidity, and helplessness had no place in the wilderness. The frontier woman had to manage the farm for days and even weeks at a time all by herself, caring for livestock, the crops, her children, and even fending off Indians. Society's concept of the marriageable woman changed to the strong woman, the woman with determination and character, and "the stereotype of the old maid shifted from the British picture of the manlike spinster who had a tom cat and preferred her nephews to the mild little woman who kept female cats and preferred her nieces." [12] The change in society's concept of the marriageable woman was accompanied by a change in the stereotype of the single woman.

But was the relationship between these two changes mere concurrence or was it cause and effect? Does society's concept of the marriageable woman affect her concept of the single woman, so that when the first changes, the second must also necessarily change? To answer this question it is necessary to consider in detail one of the changes that has been made in the stereotype of the single woman and the corresponding change in the social image of the marriageable woman.

Dorothy Deegan has made a sociological study of the stereotype of the single woman in 394 important American novels from 1820 to 1935. Her study describes society's picture of the single woman in this period. [13] Deegan says that the novel is second only to the "stage as the most liberal of all media in presenting minority characters

---

[11]   Mead, *Male and Female*, p. 303.

[12]   *Ibid.*

[13]   Deegan, *op. cit.* Admittedly, novels sometimes give an exaggerated picture of society. Also, their viewpoint is onesidedly masculine since most authors are men. Yet, the assumption that social attitudes are accurately reflected in fiction has scientific support. Literature is a cultural product that inevitably partakes of the spirit of its times. One of the more important studies supporting the assumption is a doctoral dissertation by James Barnett, *Divorce and the American Divorce Novel 1858—1937: A Study in Literary Reflections of Social Influences,* Philadelphia, privately printed, 1939, quoted by Deegan, pp. 26 and 187. However, some restrictions must be placed on the use of fiction as reflections of social attitudes. First, the social thinking of creative writers is often several years ahead of social fact. Cf. Deegan, pp. 125, 126. Secondly, novels reflect the attitudes of society as a whole, but not of every segment of society.

sympathetically and honestly," [14] and yet the novel makes extensive use of a stereotype of the single woman. [15] With respect to the single woman the novel still reflects the attitudes and evaluation of the man on the street.

The awareness of the existence and the pattern of this stereotype is so widespread that authors are conscious that they are dealing with a stereotype when they characterize a single woman; but they use it nevertheless. Edna Ferber, for example, describes two older unmarried women in these words: the "two women were incredibly drawn in the pattern of the New England spinster of fiction." [16]

Deegan discovered that although single women appear frequently in American novels, nearly always they are minor characters. Life does not revolve around them. They are not important to the drama of life and progress of history. [17] In many instances their names are quaint or odd, suggesting that single women are such, because the author's choice of names is not arbitrary but used as a means of characterization. [18] Generally, the single woman is represented as lacking ambition to change her economic and social statuses, which are nearly always very low. The single woman has no ambition for herself. [19] As a result, circumstances are seldom frustrating and neither success nor failure is conspicuously present in her life. [20] When failure is expressed, it is usually failure to marry. When success is expressed, it is success in helping another succeed. Though single women often take an active part in community affairs, it is usually as "purveyors of gossip." Their lives are so empty of importance and interest that, like parisites, they use the lives of others. Otherwise their interests are limited to a few individuals or only to themselves. [21] With few exceptions they have either no vocation or a modest, humble one. The few who do have important vocations show little superior ability or success. [22] In a majority of cases they get along well with others but, characteristically, because they are not dynamic enough to clash with anyone. [23] Only eight of the 150 single women characters in this group of novels have an unconventional sex relationship. Most of the rest are sexless creatures. [24] In one-third of the novels some admiration is shown for the unmarried woman, but the admiration is never strong and is always directed toward some quality of her character, never toward her

14   Deegan, *op. cit.*, p. xiii.
15   *Ibid.*, p. 111.
16   *So Big*, New York, Penguin Books, 1947, p. 4.
17   *Op. cit.*, p. 85.
18   *Ibid.*
19   *Ibid.*, p. 87.
20   *Ibid.*, p. 89.
21   *Ibid.*, p. 90.
22   *Ibid.*, pp. 92, 93.
23   *Ibid.*, pp. 94, 95.
24   *Ibid.*, p. 96.

singleness. Singleness is always felt to be a lack, a shortcoming, a failure, something to be avoided at nearly any cost. Not one is envied because of the freedom from responsibility provided by her singleness. In the other two-thirds of the novels the attitudes are, in this order of prevalence, pity, ridicule, and indifference. [25]

The single woman is referred to as "old maid," "spinster," "old hag," "silly old ass," "poor old thing," "old cat," and "foolish old girl." [26] Her adjustment to singleness follows the general pattern of apathy, resignation, and reticence. Usually the unmarried woman effects no change of personality or status in the story. She only makes the best of a bad situation. [27]

The resultant image from these characterizations is of a somewhat admirable individual, who is yet more often pitied or ridiculed than admired. She is altruistic and decorous in behavior but also mousy, homely, gossiping, of lowly social position, and dependent upon the financial and emotional support of others. This was society's concept of the single woman in the period 1820–1935. Edna Ferber, an author known for her sociological insights, describes this stereotype of the single woman: "mitts, preserves, Bible, chilly best room, solemn and kittenless cat, order, little-girls-mustn't . . . [smelling] of apples—of withered apples that have rotted at the core . . . , all black and mouldy at . . . heart." [28]

This stereotype was found in American novels written before 1935, but it has not disappeared from the American scene. In novels written since then "one finds certain variations on the old themes, a further extension of some of the newer ones, but also a persistence of the stereotype with little or no variation." [29] The single woman is still described as the "poor childless, chickless, figless Miss Dove! She was Woman Bereft." [30]

Although the 1820–1935 stereotype still crops up today, provoking ridicule or pity, within the past two decades an important change in the social attitude toward the single woman and in the underlying stereotype has begun to emerge. In recent years the married woman is seen as financially secure, socially acceptable, and personally well-adjusted, but the single woman is seen as bitter, sour, and warped. [31] The distinguished sociologist Margaret Mead also recognizes this change: society today will not "treat the woman who is not chosen with the simple pity accorded the wall flower of a century ago. Less kindly

---

25   *Ibid.*, p. 102.
26   *Ibid.*, p. 105.
27   *Ibid.*, p. 110.
28   *Loc. cit.*
29   Deegan, *op. cit.*, p. 166.
30   Frances Patton, *Good Morning, Miss Dove,* New York, Dodd, Mead and Company, 1954, p. 48.
31   George H. Preston, *The Substance of Mental Health,* quoted by Deegan, *op. cit.*, p. 186.

verdicts—'She must be neurotic,' 'She doesn't pay attention,' 'She hasn't made the most of her chances'—come all too easily to the lips" of society. [32] In the last few decades the new stereotype of the neurotic, sexually starved old maid, has come to the fore. The single woman is no longer the mild, mousy, dull, ineffective, sexless creature. She has become the emotionally warped, sour, maladjusted, neurotic daughter of the neurotic mother.

This new social picture of the single woman varies in its details, but the variation is only a variation of types of neuroses. However, the cause of the unmarried woman's neurotic attitudes and actions is always thought to be her frustrated sex drive: society sees her as neurotic because she does not have a normal sex life. In its specifics the stereotype varies from the repressed neurotic to the obsessed neurotic. She may have repressed her sexual instinct and become the prim, prudish, queer trouble-maker who is cruel but cannot help being so. She has killed all the vitality she may once have had. As one novelists sketches her, "she looks like somebody's old-maid aunt . . . . I'd as soon get into bed with a stepladder." [33] This is the sexually frigid woman. Or the satisfaction of the sex instinct may be an obsession with the single woman. The mildest form of this "old-maid" type is the woman who lives with the eternal hope of satisfying her desire. She does not go out seeking sexual satisfaction, but she never gives up the hope that it will come to her. This variation of the new stereotype has so penetrated the social consciousness that it has caused a change in the "old-maid" jokes. The "old maid" still researches under her bed before she goes to sleep at night to see if a man is there, but motivated by hope, not fear. [34] She is the woman who is "afraid to confess the sordid fact of her own chastity"—a thing a woman would not tell her own mother or she would have her analyzed. [35] The most overt form of the sexually obsessed single woman is found in the social picture of the woman who takes her sex when, where, and how she can find it. She is the predatory animal. She is described in recent American fiction as the man-crazy, hard-bitten woman who wears sequin-decorated dresses and always smells of raw gin, the woman who engages in illicit affairs with an alarming frequency, whether heterosexual or homosexual.

Modern society tends to see the single woman as neurotic; regardless of the type of her neurotic reaction it is linked to her abnormal sex life. Even if her behavior is not overtly sexual, the fundamental cause

---

[32]   Op. cit., pp. 325, 326.

[33]   Henry Bellaman, King's Row, quoted by Deegan, op. cit., p. 178. The above summary of the changed stereotype of the single woman is based on pp. 165—179 of Deegan's book.

[34]   A typical example: An old maid told her friend one morning, "Last night as I was going to sleep, I thought I heard a noise under my bed, but when I turned on the flashlight, I was under there all alone."

[35]   Dawn Powell, A Time to Be Born, Quoted by Deegan, op. cit., pp. 175, 176.

[36]   Deegan, op. cit., p. 173.

of her queerness is sexual. She is the one who let her chance slip by and forgot that "even fourteen kids in a boxcar, ... with female trouble thrown in, has its points," [37] if one is seeking to live the full life.

Many elements in the old stereotype are fading away. For example, the characteristic of financial dependence, very clear and strong in the old stereotype, is being soft-pedaled or even ignored. Again, there is reason to believe that this change is related to a changed concept of marriage. Before the first world war the financial security of marriage was one of its important benefits for women, for there were few opportunities to find this security outside of marriage. Therefore, the single woman was seen as destitute: "Not for her the consolation and rest of a husband's protection.... Lonely, uncared for, she often, even in old age, must battle for existence, with no loving hand to lighten her cares." [38] But when women became a generally accepted part of the working force and when their wages rose, the financial benefit of marriage lost its significance, the characteristic of financial dependence began to fade from the stereotype of the single woman.

In spite of the change in the stereotype of the single woman the social attitude toward her is noticeably persistent. Society judges her not as an individual but as one of a class—as an old maid. Regardless of the nature of her occupation, her good deeds, and her personal qualities she is neither wholly satisfying nor wholly commendable. Society believes that the unmarried woman is unsuccessful in her attempt to be a complete woman even though she must do a man's work and live a man's life. Therefore, society assumes that she has a deep loneliness, a nagging dissatisfaction, or a nameless unrest. If the single woman is saved from social ridicule, it is usually by pity. The basic attitude is still derogatory. Whether the older single woman is seen as dull, resigned to a life of pettiness, decorous and conventional in behavior or as neurotic, bitter, and domineering, what person would wish to emulate her?

The change in the stereotype of the single woman from the colorless, sexless, dehydrated creature to the neurotic, sex-hungry female is caused by a new, psychological interpretation of life. Theodor Reik calls the present, the "psychological era." The single woman, marriage, the married woman, the marriageable woman—all are psychologically evaluated. [39] Central in this psychological evaluation is the sexual evaluation. In common parlance psychological interpretation means the discovery and analysis of sexual desires, sexual inhibitions, traumas which affect sexual behavior, and so forth. The recent change to a psychological interpretation, often with the same emphasis on the sexual cause, is found in other stereotypes: the villain has become the problem drinker,

---

[37]   Fannie Hurst, *Lonely Parade*, quoted by Deegan, *op. cit.*, p. 179.

[38]   Adele Crepaz, *The Emancipation of Women*, London, Swan Sonnenschein, 1893, p. 82.

[39]   *Of Love and Lust*, p. 372.

the invalid wife the maladjusted neurotic, and the harping mother-in-law a case of arrested development. In the psychological era the sexual deviations of the unmarried woman are made more commonplace and more understandable. She is still defined in terms of her singleness, but singleness is now interpreted sexually.

There is good reason for concluding that the new stereotype of the single woman, now evolving in the public consciousness, is the result of the new sexual concept of marriage. Within the past few decades an awareness of the influence of sexuality upon the personality has begun to emerge in American society. It has influenced education, religion, literature, and even the structure of society. The discussion of sex is no longer limited to biology classes. Courses in sociology, psychology, literature, marriage counseling, marketing, advertising, and creative writing are being reoriented with a new emphasis on the central role of sex. All the various fields of human activity related to these subjects now take cognizance of the influence of the sex drive upon the reactions, choices, attitudes, and prejudices of man. The men who manufacture and sell automobiles, clothing, perfumes, household articles, cigars, and even heavy machinery take into account the sexual connotations of their products. Novels, movies, and drama all have their "sex angle." Words such as repression, fixation, neurotic, homosexual, nymphomaniac, sublimation, and libido have become more or less common in the everyday vocabulary. The Victorian innocence of sexuality has lost its hold on the social mind. The modern awareness of sexuality is especially evident in society's concept of marriage. Marriage is still seen as a legal relationship, a social relationship, an economic relationship, but the emphasis has shifted to marriage as a sexual relationship. The new emphasis upon the sexual aspect is evident both in society's concept of the qualifications necessary for marriage and in her concept of the consequences and benefits of marriage.

Sex appeal has superseded many other factors as an attractive force for marriage. A woman is seldom a good marriage prospect unless she coy, flirtatious, and physically appealing. The Victorian maiden's test-question to her suitor, "If you had to choose, would you take the upper or lower half of me?" is now an absurdity. Society regards sexual qualifications as having great importance for marriage. The significance of these sexual qualifications is not limited to satisfactory coitus. Sexual compatibility is seen as one of the chief requirements for a happy, well-adjusted marriage because it is considered basic to harmony in all the other aspects of the relationship. If the sexual relationship is disturbed, the whole marriage relationship is affected. Everything from wife-beating to neglect of children is traced to an unsatisfactory sex life. Therefore, marriage manuals have become sex manuals and premarital counseling has become simply sex instruction.

Equally as important as the redefinition of the qualifications is the redefinition of the benefits of marriage. The regular and complete satisfaction of the sex instinct is equated with healthy sex life. Probably as the result of the permeation of Freudian psychology into the public consciousness the regular and complete satisfaction of the sex drive is considered a prerequisite for a well-adjusted and successful personality. This satisfaction is thus an important goal and one of the chief benefits of marriage. The sexual qualifications and benefits were never totally absent from the social evaluation of marriage, but previously they did not have such prominence, nor were they seen as so basic to all the other aspects of marriage. Prior to the past few decades Victorian prudishness relegated the sexual aspect of marriage to an inferior position and almost denied its infuence upon the various other aspects of life.

It is important to remember that the above is a description only of social attitude. The actual qualifications necessary for a successful marriage and the real benefits and results of marriage are not under consideration. To determine the relation between the social attitude toward the single woman and the social concept of marriage, the actual consequences of marriage are of little importance. In actual fact, marriage may give a high degree of economic security, but if society is not aware of this benefit or places little or no value on economic security, the fact will have no appreciable influence upon the social attitude toward marriage and upon the related social stereotype of the unmarried woman.

There are many other requirements and benefits of marriage besides the sexual; but the sexual looms largest in the American social mind. The new sexual concept of marriage has affected the stereotype of the single woman is stereotyped as an economic and social failure. In an when the economic and social benefits of marriage are prominent in the public consciousness—as they were in the period 1820—1935—the single woman is stereotyped as an economic and social failure. In an age when the sexual qualifications of marriage are strongly emphasized—as they are today—the single woman is seen as a sexual failure. She is apriorily judged as being too strongly bound to her father, her mother, or her own sex, as repressed, or as a case of arrested development because of a childhood trauma. She is seen as sexually unqualified for marriage. This sexual deficiency has broad implications for it is the root of all her personal and social shortcomings. Society thinks that the unmarried woman's virginity is the cause of her oddness. [40] Society tends to interpret every "harsh word, every scold, every sign of irritation, as an effect of virginity." [41] Today, a woman's failure to marry means she has "missed the crowning experience of life," the right to motherhood, the chance of loving a man and being loved by him, and the right to sexual gratification. [42] She is one of society's

---

[40]   John Laurence, *The Single Woman*, New York, Duell, Sloan and Pearce, 1952, pp. 53—70.

[41]   *Ibid.*, p. 113.

[42]   M. B. Smith, *The Single Woman of Today*, London, Watts, 1951, p. 5.

handicapped because she does not have what is rightfully hers, what she needs for the full life, a husband and a child. As a result the single woman has been stereotyped as the sexually frustrated neurotic.

This description of the sexual aspect of marriage is not the whole of contemporary society's concept of marriage. Nor is the sexual aspect of singleness the only determinative of the social concept of the unmarried woman. Many other aspects of marriage receive social recognition and are socially valued. But in the mind of present society the sexual aspect of marriage is central.

After examining the details of society's stereotype of the single woman in the period 1820—1935 and the concept of marriage in that age, and after examining the details of the stereotype in post-1935 society and its concept of marriage, it can reasonably be concluded that the social evaluation of the older unmarried woman is directly linked to the social evaluation of marriage. [43] In both periods the stereotype of the single woman is the inverse of society's concept of the marriageable and the married woman. Whenever society changes its idea of the qualities necessary for marriage or of the personal benefits resulting from marriage, the stereotype of the single woman changes to one which is the inverse of the new qualifications and benefits. When, as in the heritage of many early American settlers, the marriageable and the married woman were thought of as gracious, charming, and dependent, the single woman was stereotyped as masculine, strong, and self-sufficient. Marriage was conceived primarily as a relationship which offered security and protection. Later, in the frontier days, the marriageable woman was self-sufficient and adaptable and the single woman was stereotyped as weak, dependent, and mild. Today, the marriageable and the married woman are seen as sexually attractive, personable, psychically mature and well-developed; and the single woman is stereotyped as homely, sexually frustrated, maladjusted, and neurotic. The single woman is always seen as lacking the qualities necessary for the pattern of marriage of each age.

What causes this inverse evaluation? Why is marital status such an important standard for society's evaluation of the single woman? Why are not the same standards used as those in the evaluation of the single man: his personal achievements, his personal qualities, and his contributions to the general welfare? What assumption is latent in this inverse evaluation? The validity of the social permise which links the concept of marriage and the evaluation of the single woman must be judged. Only then can it be determined whether the social problem of the single woman is to be solved by changing the standard of society or by obviating the causes of deviation from the standard.

---

[43] Reik concurs in this conclusion. He gives several other examples of changes in society's concept of marriage which produced corresponding changes in society's concept of the single woman. Cf. *Of Love and Lust*, pp. 369—371.

The Basic Presupposition Producing Society's Attitude and Evaluation

The problem of the unmarried woman is actually the problem of woman in general. Society demands of a woman marriage and parenthood in a way and to a degree that it does not demand of man. The obligation to marry and to become a mother is not merely one of many obligations for woman; it is in society's judgment one of the most important of her obligations: it is almost an absolute obligation. This obligation is so great and so universal that the unmarried woman, regardless of the cause of her singleness, is socially censured. Throughout her life her marital status is immediately identified by the title "Miss" and she is tagged with the term "old maid" and all its derogatory connotations. She has willingly or unwillingly transgressed one of society's unwritten laws. Many and varied are the reasons given for this imperative: some say that woman must marry because she was created for man; others because only in marriage and motherhood can she be truly feminine; or, only in these relationships can she find true peace and happiness; only in this way can she avoid mental illness; or, this is the way a woman truly serves God.

The age-old emphasis upon the marital and parental obligation of woman came to its clearest expression in modern times in the Femininist Controversy. Adele Crepaz, one of the foremost leaders of the opposition—whose book was published with a commendatory introduction by W. E. Gladstone—sounded the cry "To me there is no more sublime, elevating spectacle in the whole world than that of a mother, who gives herself up to the fulfillment of her duties. *No other aim should be placed before her sex.*" [44]

Beginning at birth the attention of the American girl is focused upon marriage and motherhood as her role in life. She plays with doll houses, toy washing machines, and kitchen utensils. She is given dolls to wash, dress, love, and care for in imitation of her mother. As she grows older, she is taught domestic, so-called feminine, duties. She is taught to be coy and winsome in order to attract the attention of boys. Her fairy tales end "and they lived happily ever after." Beyond the first few years of life it is not what she does that receives the highest praise, but what she is: little boys are praised for how fast they can run, how strong they are, how they can "beat up any kid in the block," but little girls for how charming, beautiful, gracious, and personable they are. The achievements and abilities of girls that do receive praise are usually related to the realization of her connubial and maternal potentials: her mathematical ability is valued because she is expected to manage a household budget someday; her shorthand and typing abilities are esteemed because she is expected to work for a few years before and possibly after marriage to help finance her new home. The short stories

---

[44] *Op. cit.,* p. 42.

she reads, the drama she hears on the radio and sees in movies and on television, the advertisements aimed at her all sum up the duty of woman as "Find a husband and live happily ever after." Attractive clothes, cosmetics, hope chests, good dating manners—all these are important for the American girl. Although this life-long training for her marital and maternal role is both natural and desirable—since it will be the role of the vast majority of women and will demand the greater share of their time, energy, and attention—the focused concentration upon marriage as *the* feminine role in life tends to make it an absolute imperative in the mind of the American girl and in the mind of society generally. Society demands that in nearly all its literature the pretty, attractive, witty girl must not be left unmarried; if she is, all is not well with the world. The American girl is trained with such singleness of purpose that if she never marries and has a family, she, as well as the rest of society, considers her life a failure. Mariage and motherhood are essential to feminine success.

The age of the "vamp" is past. The publicity for stage and screen personalties emphasizes their happy home life and their concern for their home and children. If a woman must choose between a career and a home, society applauds the decision to abandon the career. A career a woman can do without, but not a family.

Success is very important for the American. It is adored, envied, enjoyed vicariously, striven for, and enjoined. Mothers search yearningly for signs that John or Mary will make good. Success is the standard of social evaluation in America, says Margaret Mead, [45] not hereditary rights or position, not education, not sexual attractiveness, not good taste and pleasant manners, not even money, in and of itself. These factors are valued only as means to or badges of success. But "Success for a woman means success in finding and keeping a husband. This is much more true than it was a generation ago, when men were still supposed to do the seeking, and some women found their new freedom outside the home so intoxicating that they could abandon themselves to their work." [46] Regardless of her other achievements, a woman has failed in life if she has not accomplished this goal.

Therefore, American society has the strange situation that as more and more women work, women in general seem less and less interested in professional success and the preparation it demands. The opening of new fields of activity for the woman has not changed society's concept of her prime obligation. The femininist struggle for the rights of women in politics, business, social work, and the natural sciences has made no measurable impact upon the social premise concerning the primary purpose of woman. When the battle had been won, society still said, "the woman's place is the home, although we will allow her to participate

45 *Male and Female*, pp. 307, 308.
46 *Ibid.*, pp. 323, 324.

in activities outside the home at the same time." Although woman in the past fifty years gained many new functions, she lost none of her old ones. The working woman is still expected to be a homemaker, a wife, and mother. [47] Since marriage is the purpose given to woman, "whether her husband is satisfactory or not, a married woman, nevertheless, shows to the world the contented face of a human being who has arrived." [48]

Professional success is even a hindrance to a woman's marital possibilities. A 1946 public opinion survey by *Fortune* magazine [49] asked men whether they would prefer a girl who had never had a job, one who had had a job and had been moderately successful, or one who had held a job and had been extremely successful. Only 21.5 per cent preferred the girl who had been extremely successful. The majority of the others answering chose the girl who had been moderately successful. The more successful a woman is professionally, the more most men fear she will not be a successful wife. The resultant picture is of a society which throws its doors open to women in nearly every field but interprets their success in these fields as damaging to their chances of marriage.

Women are part of this society and share its attitudes and expectations. Culture or society is no omnipotent, arbitrary potentate assigning roles and aims to classes and groups. Society is no autonomous being that forces woman into a position against her will. As Viola Klein reminds Margaret Mead, society is not the *prima causa*, for the "problem remains: Who created the Creator." [50] The concepts and attitudes of society are concepts and attitudes of man *and* women.

Therefore, the American girl, too, sees marriage as *the* desired goal in life. "A half-century ago the eyes of the specially able girl who went to college faced ahead towards a career. The idea of marriage was often pushed aside as a handicap. To-day, the girl of the same ability is usually willing to admit that she wants to marry, and seems more willing to sacrifice her career to marriage than to sacrifice a chance for marriage to her career .... If [girls] have brains and ability, sheer virtuousity plus the need to succeed may lead them to become engrossed in their work, but seldom so engrossed that the desire for marriage is blocked out." [51] Marriage is still the first desire of the American girl. She sees it as the only way to real, lasting happiness for a woman—in concurrence with the rest of society. Any service or accomplishment outside marriage is, at best, only a second-rate substitute.

Klein suggests that society's strong emphasis upon the marital role as *the* purpose of woman stems in a large measure from the agricultural

---

[47]   Klein, *op. cit.*, p. 33.
[48]   Harding, *op. cit.*, p. 137.
[49]   "Women in America," October, 1946, p. 8.
[50]   *Op. cit.*, p. 139.
[51]   Mead, *Male and Female*, p. 323.

and industrial revolution. [52] Before these social changes there was hardly any job that was not also performed by women. The home was the unit of production and the wife as well as the unmarried daughter, sister, or aunt was a valuable contributor to the productive capacity of the family. Woman, married or unmarried, had an economic significance and purpose. The general attitude is expressed in the advice given in *A Present for a Servant Maid,* published in 1743: "You cannot expect to marry in such a manner as neither of you shall have occasion to work and none but a fool will take a wife whose bread must be earned solely by his labour and who will contribute nothing towards it herself." [53] But the industrial and agricultural revolution separated the home and industry; society became sufficiently productive to dispense with the help of women; and a non-productive female section of the family became a badge of social success. The result was that the marital and maternal obligations of women received more and more emphasis. Marriage became increasingly an advantage for woman and a liability for man. The unmarried state was increasingly regarded as a freedom and opportunity for man, but a limitation, failure, and loss for woman; for outside marriage she lacked a socially approved role.

It is very important to notice that when American society says "the woman's place is the home," it is not reducing woman to a sexual and reproductive being. The social problem of the unmarried woman cannot be solved by pointing out she is more than this. Society does not say that the purpose of the wife is merely the physical gratification of the husband and the bearing of children. This street-corner concept of the purpose of woman is fading from American society as the influence of the middle class and its standards and ideals spread. The spread is rapid and already extensive in American society. [54] The mere accomplishment of marriage and reproduction is not the fulfillment of woman's purpose. She is seen as more than a potential companion and sexual partner of man and a mother of his children. The role of wife and mother is a social, psychological, educational, religious, financial, and political role. Only when she accepts these responsibilities is she considered a good wife and mother. Margaret Mead makes the accurate observation "America [is] not Europe, where women had been expected to do more praying than the men but not to take any responsibility outside the home." [55]

In America women are not only allowed but encouraged to go out into public life and take an active part. The woman who has time only for her home is likely to be stigmatized as incompetent, or financially unsuccessful or shiftless. [56] The American woman is expected to have

---

[52]   *Op. cit.,* pp. 9, 10.
[53]   Quoted by Klein, *op. cit.,* p. 9.
[54]   *Ibid.,* p. 281.
[55]   *Male and Female,* p. 303.
[56]   *Ibid.,* p. 307.

"outside interests and activities." Her duty to society and to her home is not complete without these activities. But, significantly, these activities are part of her role as wife and mother. The part she takes in public life is as a representative of the home and its interests. All her other activities are socially approved as correlaries of her duty as wife and mother. Therefore, it is not accurate to say simply that the only duty of woman is to marry and have children. She is expected to be a psychologist and educator to train her children; a nurse, dietitian, and cook to care for the health of her children; a citizen active in politics, PTA, and community affairs to provide for the social welfare of her family; and an active church member for her family's religious welfare. But apart from marriage these activities lose much of their social significance. The unmarried professional woman doing social work, psychiatry, or political work is still stigmatized because she has failed to make that contribution which society demands of her as a woman: she has not become a wife and a mother.

Marriage is often considered such a central and important obligation of woman that it becomes the primary purpose of her existence. Her goal and destiny in life can be realized only through marriage. Men, too, are expected to marry, and most men do. Marriage is seen as an obligation of man and one that is important for himself and for society, but it is not seen as the purpose of man. Therefore, single women, but not single men, are classified as a "supernumerary class" of society. [57]

A woman's marital and parental status is the standard by which society judges her value and importance. Therefore, the modern girl finds it so easy to sacrifice her career for marriage; literature continually presents the joy of feminine surrender of personal ideals and aspirations to the ideals and aspirations of the man, through marriage; the unmarried woman is so severely judged and not the unmarried man; the stereotype of the single woman is the inverse reflection of society's evaluation of the requirements and benefits of marriage; success for a woman is defined as marriage; and professional success endangers a woman's chances of marriage. Socially considered, woman gains her greatest importance through marriage. Outside this relationship her existence is senseless and a failure.

This concept is a common thesis even of books and articles on the unmarried woman. M. B. Smith in her book *The Single Woman of Today* argues "the right to motherhood, ... [the] chance of loving a man and being loved by a man, ... [and the] right to sex gratification ... are fundamental needs of self-fulfillment, and therefore of mental health. ..." [58] From this she concludes "No civilization can change a Woman's inherent role." [59] This statement shows little change

---

[57]   *Ibid.*, p. 304.
[58]   P. 5.
[59]   P. 6.

from that of Adele Crepaz sixty years earlier: *"If women are to be protected from mental disturbance and from disappointed lives, let us preserve our gifted, clever sisters for the sanctity of domestic life."* [60] Consequently, *"No other aim should be placed before her sex."* [61] W. Gallichan in *The Great Unmarried* concurs, "The compulsory celibate is cheated of a supreme human right. This injustice is visited by Nature with unflinching severity, and the individual and the community are rigorously punished." [62] Those authors who seek the solution to the social problem of the older unmarried woman in the removal of those factors which prevent her from marrying—such as an oversupply of women, psychic blocks in both men and women, and the economic liability of marriage for men—share the same presupposition: that all women should marry. Amram Scheinfeld, for example, suggests as a solution to the social problem of millions of women "doomed to spinsterhood," the providing of greater incentives to men to marry and the reduction of the male death rate. [63] J. H. Kohlbrugge in his work *Practische Sociologie* operates from the same presupposition and arrives at similar conclusions. He says the first and natural destiny of the woman is marriage and parenthood. Therefore, the proper way to solve the social problem of the unmarried woman is to help her marry, by bettering the life of man to decrease the oversupply of women, by developing in girls that which is typically feminine in order to attract husbands, and by halting the universal education of girls for other tasks. [64]

The use of marital and parental status as a standard for measuring the value and importance of woman is common even to many in American society who see her ultimate purpose as lying beyond becoming a wife and a mother. The Christian church affirms that woman's purpose, as well as man's, is the service of God. Yet, Emil Brunner says, [65] especially in Christian circles marriage is seen as the only way to the realization of her earthly purpose. Protestantism, because of its reaction to the monastic ideal, has both in theory and in practice made the unmarried state ethically contemptible. Whether one sees marriage and motherhood as the ultimate purpose or as the only means through which a woman can achieve her ultimate purpose, the social evaluation of the older unmarried woman is essentially the same—she is a failure as a human being.

---

[60]   *Op. cit.*, p. 122.

[61]   *Ibid.*, p. 42.

[62]   London, T. Werner Laurie, [1916], p. 10.

[63]   *Women and Men,* New York, Harcourt, Brace, 1944, pp. 191—196 and 391—396.

[64]   Groningen, Wolters, 1927, Vol. 5, pp. 1, 2 and 26, 27.

[65]   *The Divine Imperative,* London, Lutterworth Press, 1937, p. 365.

Biblical Judgment of Society's Presupposition

In seeking the solution to the social problem of the unmarried woman many writers trace the various causes of a woman's remaining single and suggest ways of counteracting these causes. However, behind this approach lies an implicit acceptance of the ideal which society uses as a standard to evaluate single women. The first step in the solution of the social problem is the examination and judgment of the ideal itself.

Is there a universal, absolute obligation of woman to marry and raise a family? Is marriage and motherhood, if not the final purpose or woman, at least the necessary requirement for the realization of her final purpose? Is marriage the one duty which no woman may avoid? In whatever form the obligation is stated, it is in essence a religious presupposition. Even sociologists who approach the social problem of the single woman from a pragmatic point of view—what is useful and good for the individual and the community—are making a religious judgment on the basis of a religious apriori: what is the purpose of man and of mankind? The standard used by society must be measured by that norm of faith and life which stands in judgment over not only individuals but kingdoms, governments, societies, and eras—the Word of God.

When the church judges a standard of society, she is always including her own self in the judgment. Each individual member of the church is also a member of the broader society and inevitably to some degree reflects the ideals and attitudes of that society. Faith does not make a person immune to social influences. The attitudes and ideals which the church shares with the rest of society affect her ministry to the unmarried woman, whether the ministry is done through the special offices or the general office of believer.

Since the goal of the church's ministry to the individual includes the promotion of a life directed according to the revealed will of God, every obligation which society presupposes and every standard with which society measures man or woman, must be judged by the revealed will of God. If woman has a universal, absolute obligation to marry, the church must use every legitimate means to promote willing conformity to this imperative and to provide the possibility of this conformity. If woman has no such obligation, the church must seek to root out this social assumption, to prevent its being used as a measure of woman, and to overcome the single woman's personal sense of failure; for this sense can block her own happiness and her own realization of her final purpose—a life dedicated to the service of God. The Biblical passages which state the woman's place and purpose in creation, her role in the kingdom, the spiritual significance of marriage, and the legitimacy and value of the unmarried state must be considered— in so far as they bear on the presupposition that every woman must marry.

The first two chapters of Genesis provide the foundation for a Biblical anthropology. Here is the basis for all further statements of the nature and destiny of mankind in general and of woman in particular: of the divine purpose of woman, of her true significance, and of her place in marriage. Genesis 1 : 26—28 records the creation of the human race and the first mandate given it. Man, male and female, was created in the image of God, and man, male and female, was commanded to "be fruitful, and multiply, and replenish the earth, and subdue it." This command was directed to mankind, not just to the male member of the race. Nowhere in this passage is there a distinction made between the task of woman and the task of man. Neither is there a separation between a cultural and a procreative task. The woman's task is not limited to procreation. She, no less than the man, is commanded to subdue the earth, [66] and man, no less than woman, was commanded to be fruitful and multiply. The subjugation of creation can be accomplished only through procreation, through a larger population to inhabit the earth and to make possible the division of labor necessary for the building of a culture. And, on the other hand, the procreative aspect of the mandate can be realized only through the subjugation of creation; for a large population demands for survival animal husbandry, agriculture, social regulations, and many other cultural products. Also, the lordship over creation includes man's dominion over his own body, as part of creation, in the task of procreation. Just as subjugation is impossible without procreation, so procreation is impossible without subjugation. The procreative task and the cultural task are two aspects of one mandate, not two diverse commands which can be separated.

Nor is either aspect directed exclusively to one sex, although one sex may play a greater role than the other in the fulfillment of one of the aspects. The burden of the procreative aspect of the mandate, for example, falls on the woman, since she must devote to it the greater part of her time, energy, and attention both before and after the birth of a child. Since the woman is preoccupied with the procreative aspect of the mandate, the burden of the cultural task falls upon the man. But neither task is limited to the one sex. Just as man is involved in the procreative task, so is woman in the cultural task.

Genesis 1 : 26—28 does not limit the woman's task to procreation, nor does it imply that this aspect of the divine imperative is more binding for her than for man. No hint is given that marriage and parenthood is a goal and purpose of woman in a way that it is not for man. Although this mandate is given to mankind as represented by Adam and Eve, the personal obligation of each individual is not

---

[66] Cf. verse 26: God created mankind in his own image and said, "let *them* have dominion." Mankind, male and female, was given lordship over the earth. Cf. K. Dronkert, *Het Huwelijk in het Oude Testament*, Leiden, Sijthoff, 1957, pp. 22, 23.

specific here. Since the fulfillment of each aspect is the necessary condition for the fulfillment of the other, an individual's exclusive devotion to the one aspect would be instrumental in effecting mankind's fulfillment of both aspects. Therefore, a man who devotes his life to the perfection of better methods of agriculture contributes to mankind's fulfillment of both aspects of the mandate. The mandate was given just after creation was complete and stated man's relation to all of creation, including his own self. Man, male and female, was placed over creation as lord of it and was told to rule and develop it as God's appointed overseer. Of man and woman's relation to their Master and of each individual's role in the master of creation, nothing further is specified.

Genesis 2 : 18–25 is more directly pertinent to the social problem of the unmarried woman, for here the creation of man, male and female, and the relation between man and woman stands in the foreground. From the first chapter of Genesis one might come to the conclusion that masculinity and femininity are only accidental or at least incidental and not of very great significance, but not so from Genesis two. The second chapter shows that woman was created after man and out of him as a helper fit for him, *ezer kenegdo*. Woman was created as a counterpart to man, a helper fit or suitable for him, one which would be a companion able to overcome man's aloneness. [67] All of prior creation had been examined (vs. 19, 20) and none had been found who corresponded to him. So woman was created.

The creation of woman receives special emphasis in the Genesis 2 account of creation, but close examination of verses 18–25 shows that nothing is said directly or indirectly about woman's obligation to marry. Indeed, the first woman did fulfill the purpose of her creation by marrying the first man. And, only through the marriage of the first woman and the first man could the mandate given in Genesis 1 : 28 be fulfilled. Therefore man received her as bone of his bones, flesh of his flesh, the *ishshah* of the *ish*. Then, as well as today, marriage was the means through which the mandate of Genesis 1 : 28 was fulfilled.

At this point great care must be taken to avoid unwarranted conclusion. At very most, one may conclude that *mankind* has an obligation to marry in order to fulfill the mandate of Genesis 1 : 28. However, the conclusion that every individual person is so obligated is not warranted from the creation accounts of Genesis 1 and 2.

Several New Testament passages clearly state that God has not so

---

[67] The prepositional phrase *kenegdo* is not a statement of the purpose of woman, that she was created for the sake of man, but is descriptive of woman: as his counterpart she is able to overcome his aloneness. This meaning is not immediately evident in the English translations, which are often read to mean: "a suitable helper for the sake of man," making the word "suitable" modify "helper" and the preposition "for" a preposition of purpose. Cf. Dronkert, *op. cit.*, p. 25.

obligated every individual. [68] Certainly there is in Genesis one and two no reason to single out the woman as having an absolute obligation to marry. If anything, the marriage of the man and his need of human companionship is most clearly emphasized in Genesis 2 : 18—25. But this passage does not say that marriage is the only way in which the aloneness of the individual can be overcome—either the aloneness of the woman or of the man.

One other Old Testament passage must be considered, Genesis 3 : 16, since it is often understood to say that woman should marry: "To the woman he said, 'I will greatly multiply your pain in childbearing; in pain shall you bring forth children, yet [or 'and'] your desire shall be for your husband, and he shall rule over you.'" This verse may not be interpreted simply as a statement of the divinely determined purpose of woman. It is part of the curse which came upon mankind as the result of its sin. It describes the present situation in a world warped by evil: just as thorns and thistles are now in the harvest, so the woman has pain in childbearing and so her desire is for her husband and he rules over her.

The entire curse, recorded in verses 14—19, is an account of the disturbing effect of sin in the relationship of mankind and creation and in the relationship of man and woman. The disturbance in the man-woman relationship is mentioned repeatedly. [69] Their oneness is disrupted and each becomes self-directed. As a result of sin the woman no longer gives herself as a helper suitable for man, seeking to fulfill his need, but she seeks a husband for the satisfaction of her own desire. She no longer considers what she can give but what she can receive. Her husband, too, no longer accepts her as bone of his bones and flesh of his flesh, a counterpart suitable for him. Sin affects also his rule over her. The effects of sin are manifest in their estrangement from each other. In reference to Genesis 3 : 16, B. Wielenga rightly contends that after the fall the creation ordinance was sharpened to a judgment. [70] The woman's desire for a husband and the man's rule over his wife are principles laid down in creation, but sin changed the first into a self-directed drive and the second into tyranny. [71]

---

[68] Cf., e.g., Matt. 19 : 10—12 and I Cor. 7 : 8, 26, 32—35.

[69] Cf. vs. 7, 11, 12.

[70] *Ons Huwelijksformulier*, Kampen, J. H. Kok, 1909, p. 207.

[71] As is evident from above, the *vav* is read as copulative, "and," instead of adversative, "but" or "yet." The last two clauses are then part of the curse and are not simply descriptive of something laid down in creation. The structure of the pericope points to the copulative interpretation. Beginning at verse 14, God pronounces a series of destructive effects of sin, many of which are introduced by this same connective particle. Secondly, the copulative interpretation is in keeping with the general theme: the terrible effects of sin upon the fulfillment of the mandate to multiply and have dominion. Finally, the word used in the Hebrew for desire does not mean simply "wanting" or "wishing" but "seeking to gain hold of," "seeking to gain mastery of." Cf. Gen. 4 : 7, "And if you do not do

Before considering the New Testament texts related to the question of woman's obligation to marry, the change in the significance of marriage from the one dispensation to the other should be noted. Sarah, Hannah, and Elizabeth experienced their childlessness, or at least their lack of a male child, as a withholding of God's blessing. Motherhood had more than mere social significance. The propagation of the race was so very important because salvation was to come through the seed of Abraham. The soteriological importance of marriage and childbearing is suggested also by Deuteronomy 23 : 1, "He whose testicles are crushed or whose male member is cut off shall not enter the assembly of the Lord." Yet, even in the Old Testament marriage and parenthood were no absolute condition for the reception of *shalom:* "Let not the eunuch say, 'Behold, I am a dry tree.' For thus says the Lord: 'To the eunuchs who keep my sabbaths, who choose the things that please me and hold fast my covenant, I will give in my house and within my walls a monument and a name better than sons and daughters; I will give them an everlasting name which shall not be cut off." [72] Nevertheless, the eunuchs do not stand in the main stream of the *Heilsgeschichte,* for in the context of these verses they are reckoned with the "foreigners," those who are not of the seed of Abraham.

In the New Testament marriage and procreation has a very different role in the *Heilsgeschichte.* Geneologies are no longer mentioned— except at the beginning of the gospels of Matthew and Luke, but these exceptions fall into the Old Testament dispensation. Nowhere in the New Testament are all the members of a family (father, mother, and children) mentioned, except for Joseph, Mary, and Jesus and Zechariah, Elizabeth, and John. Again, these exceptions prove the point, for these two families belong to the Old Testament dispensation: they are the fulfillment of the Old Testament promises.

With the inauguration of Jesus' ministry, or more particularly, with his resurrection and with Pentecost, the new era arrived. In the rest of the New Testament the family fades from *heilsgeschichtliche* importance. The families of those who have a role in the *Heilsgeschichte* seem to be of little importance for the *heilsgeschichte* itself. The very lack of mention of families is conspicuous. Peter was married, for his mother-in-law is mentioned, but nothing is said about his wife (if she was still living) or his children (if he had any). Notice also that the Bible speaks many times of Mary and Martha, who were living with their brother Lazarus, but whether any of the three were married is

---

well, sin is couching at the door; its desire is for you, but you must master it." This desire is not that laid down in creation but an effect of sin.

Perhaps even the name Adam gives to woman in verse 20, "Eve, the mother of all living," instead of *ishshah,* the counterpart of man, is an attempt to lower her to an instrument, as C. M. van Asch van Wijck suggests in *Tweezaam is de Mens,* Amsterdam, W. ten Have, 1950, pp. 37—39.

[72]   Isaiah 56 : 3b, 4.

not mentioned. Paul repeatedly names women who were co-laborers with him in the gospel, [73] but with only a few exceptions he never mentions their husbands or children, although it would be very unlikely that all these were unmarried. The few times that the family is specifically mentioned in the New Testament are accounts of baptisms. [74] The New Testament significance of the family seems to be limited largely to this sacrament.

There is correspondence as well as difference between the New and Old Testaments. Marriage and parenthood are honored and in some circumstances expressly advocated in the New Testament too. The author of Hebrews writes, "Let marriage be held in honor among all." [75] In Ephesians 5 : 21–33 Paul compares the relation of husband to that of Christ and his church. [76] When writing to Timothy, Paul denounces those who forbid marriage as "deceitful spirits" and "liars." [77] To the Corinthians he writes, "if you marry, you do not sin." [78] Under some circumstances Paul expressly advocates marriage: "So I would have the younger widows marry, bear children, rule their households, and give the enemy no occasion to revile us." [79] The New Testament does not represent marriage as an evil state nor as insignificant for the Christian life, but as an intimate relationship to be desired as the immediate source of spiritual blessings. It is a holy relationship in and through which a man and a woman can honor and serve God.

The question of the New Testament significance of the marriage relationship can be answered only by placing it in the larger context of the New Testament significance of all earthly relationships. How important are the relationships of parent and child, of husband and wife, of ruler and subject, and of master and slave? They are not inconsequential. Our citizenship in a heavenly kingdom [80] does not cancel our obligations to earthly kingdoms; [81] nor does freedom in Christ rescind the obligations of a slave to his master, [82] nor does equality before Christ [83] wipe out the wife's duty to submit to her husband. [84] For the Christian these relationships continue, and they remain significant for his life. In a sense, they determine his Christian duty in given situations, for what he does to another, he is doing to

---

[73] Cf., e.g., Rom. 16 and Phil. 4.
[74] Cf. Acts 16 : 33.
[75] Heb. 13 : 4.
[76] Cf. also II Cor. 11 : 2, Rev. 19 : 7, and Rev. 22 : 17.
[77] I Tim. 4 : 1–3.
[78] I Cor. 7 : 28.
[79] I Tim. 5 : 14. Cf. also I Cor. 7 : 2.
[80] Phil. 3 : 20.
[81] Cf. Rom. 13 and I Peter 2 : 13, 14.
[82] I Cor. 7 : 21–23. Cf. also Col. 3 : 22–4 : 1 and Eph. 6 : 5–9.
[83] Col. 3 : 11 and Gal. 3 : 28.
[84] Col. 3 : 18 and Eph. 5 : 22–24.

God: honor of parents is honor of God, and sexual adultery is spiritual adultery.

Yet these relationships are not finally decisive. They do not determine a person's ultimate value and significance, nor are they the final determinant of man's obligation. Jesus loved and honored his mother, but when she stood between him and his divinely-given mission, he answered her anxious admonition, "How is it that you sought me? Did you not know that I must be in my Father's house?" [85]

The coming of Christ has relativized the significance of marriage and parenthood. The *koinonia* of the church has in part replaced the *koinonia* of the family. When Jesus' mother and brothers interrupted his preaching with a request to speak to him, Jesus asked the question, "Who is my mother, and who are my brothers?" and he added, "whoever does the will of my Father in heaven is my brother, and sister, and mother." [86] The relationship to Christ is dominant for the Christian. This singular statement of Jesus reveals also the personal responsibility of each individual to God above and distinct from his earthly relationships.

Nowhere did Jesus use stronger terms to state the secondary importance of earthly relationships than to the multitude: "If any man comes to me, and hate not his own father and mother and wife and children and brothers and sister, yes, and even his own life, he cannot be my disciple." [87] Although Jesus honored marriage in his ministry, he was also careful not to overestimate the importance of the relationship. When the Sadducees posed the question about the resurrection of the woman who married seven times, Jesus told them that they had overevaluated marriage. They had failed to see that marriage is a temporal state: "For in the resurrection they neither marry nor are given in marriage, but are like angels in heaven." [88]

Marriage has a kingdom purpose, but a temporary one that shall be fulfilled when history ends. It is the means through which God's covenant promise is realized and through which the blessings, joys, and duties of salvation come to the husband and wife. Yet it is subservient to the God-man relationship which dominates human life. Full, complete, dedicated, perfect service is possible apart from the earthly relationships of child-parent, husband-wife, and brother-sister. If the demands of these relationships conflict with the demands of the relationship to God, earthly relationships not only may but must be repudiated. Even if conflict never arises, the Christian is required to place these relationships into a proper perspective. They must not be the ultimate object of his loyalty, his first and greatest love. Emil Brunner has correctly stated, "... for one who in faith already belongs to the 'age to come,' where

---

[85]   Luke 2 : 49.
[86]   Matt. 12 : 46–50.
[87]   Luke 14 : 26.
[88]   Matt. 22 : 30.

'they neither marry nor are given in marriage,' the hope of Redemption makes it impossible to regard the order of creation: 'be fruitful and multiply,' as an absolutely binding command, while it would be utterly impossible to proclaim marriage as a universal duty, absolutely binding on every human being." [89]

It was with a clear view of man's ultimate purpose and a calm, sober, moderate evaluation of marriage and its role in the realization of this purpose that Jesus told his disciples, "there are eunuchs who have made themselves eunuchs for the sake of the kingdom of heaven. He who is able to receive this, let him receive it." [90] Marriage is no obligation for all; there are good and noble reasons for singleness.

Neither does Paul say that woman has an absolute obligation to marry, when he writes the Corinthians that woman was created *dia ton andra.* [91] When Paul says that woman was formed for the benefit of man, he says nothing about the way in which she helps her counterpart, man. This text does not warrant the conclusion that the only way woman benefits man is through marriage and parenthood. Paul is considering the man-woman relationship only in so far as it is the foundation for some rules of worship which he is advocating to the Corinthian Church, and he draws no other conclusions from it.

In I Timothy 2 : 13—15 he comes much closer to the subject considered in this chapter: "For Adam was formed first, then Eve; and Adam was not deceived, but the woman was deceived and became a transgressor. Yet woman will be saved through bearing children if she continues in faith and love and holiness, with modesty." Again in the context of providing a certain structure for the church and a certain order in her public worship services, Paul returns to the subject of the position of woman and of her obligation. But is Paul saying that a woman's salvation depends upon her marrying and her bearing of children? Paul is speaking of woman in the collective sense; [92] he is not speaking of the salvation which came through the bearing of *the Child,* Jesus, for the promise of Genesis had already been fulfilled. C. Bouma rightly finds the key to the correct understanding of this passage in the word *sothesetai.* [93] The point of this text is not that sinful woman shall be saved from eternal damnation through her becoming a mother, because at the end of the verse Paul shows he is thinking of women who are already Christian: they must *continue* in faith and love and holiness. These are women who have already been saved from damnation through

---

[89]   *The Divine Imperative,* p. 364.
[90]   Matt. 19 : 12.
[91]   I Cor. 11 : 9.
[92]   The plural verb *meinōsin* points to a collective subject of the preceding verb, *sothēsetai.*
[93]   *De Brieven van den Apostel Paulus aan Timotheus en Titus,* Amsterdam, H. A. van Bottenburg, [n.d.], p. 127.

faith. The word *sothenai*, as often in the New Testament, [94] has a positive, future significance, not a negative "saved from." It points to salvation in the fullest sense, including all its blessings, glory, happiness, and obligations. This verse then means that the act of childbearing is a spiritual blessing through Christ, just as through sin it became a curse. Paul is saying that through motherhood a woman serves and glorifies God and that through motherhood God blesses her. Motherhood has a spiritual significance and is involved in God's process of salvation and in woman's own participation in this salvation.

Yet Paul does not say that childbearing is the *only* way a woman can participate in full salvation, the only way in which she can serve God and in which God can bless her. This is no merely academic distinction. It is basic for a grasp of the Biblical concept of woman, or marriage, and of singleness. The honoring of one particular state, such as marriage, does not mean that every Christian must necessarily achieve that state. I Timothy 2 : 13—15 says nothing about an absolute obligation to marry.

Later in the history of revelation the concept of the relative importance of marriage and of singleness came to richer development in Paul's first letter to the Corinthian church. This church had sent Paul several questions about marriage, sexual intercourse, and singleness, which he answers in chapter seven. Characteristically, Paul places the questions in a larger frame of reference, that of the bearing and effect of various earthly states upon the Christian life and its obligations.

The heart of his discourse is found in verses 17—24. These verses are no excursion down a side road from the chief subject of the chapter, should a Christian live in a married state or outside it? They provide the principle by which the question can be settled. [95] The understanding of these verses is central to a grasp of the entire chapter. Although it may appear otherwise from verse 17, Paul does not say that the state of marriage or of singleness, of freedom or of slavery, of circumcision or of uncircumcision is a vocation, a calling, which each man has from the Lord. *Kaleo* means: called to be reconciled with God, called to be saved, called to be a Christian. This soteriological meaning of *kaleo* is

---

[94] Cf. J. H. Thayer, *A Greek-English Lexicon of the New Testament,* New York, American Book Company, 1889, p. 610.

[95] Therefore, the introductory words of v. 25, *peri de ton parthenon,* do not indicate a transition back to a previously broached subject but head the conclusions which Paul draws from the general rule laid down in the immediately preceding verses. This view of the chapter may possibly enlighten the puzzling statement in the rest of v. 25, "I have no commandment of the Lord, but I give my opinion as one who by the Lord's mercy is trustworthy." Paul may be saying that he has had no command from God dealing directly and specifically with the problem raised by the Corinthians, but the general principle he does have, and he is applying it to their problem as one whose judgment can be trusted through God's merciful gift of the Spirit to him.

the usual one in the epistles of Paul [96] and is certainly its meaning in verses 18, 20, 21, 22, and 24 where he speaks of being called while in these various states. The point here made is that whether one is circumcised or uncircumcised, slave or free, at the time of his conversion, he must and can live the Christian life. Circumstances and states do not have to be altered in order to be a Christian. They may be altered: in verse 15 Paul permits the separation from the unbelieving partner who no longer desires to live in the marriage relation, in verse 21 he approves the slave's obtaining freedom if he has the opportunity, and in verse 27 he permits the single person to marry. Paul could hardly approve of change if in verse 17 he meant that we are called to these states.

Neither is verse 20, "Every one should remain in that in which he was called," or verse 24, "So brethren, in whatever each was called, there let him remain with God,' the statement of a social reactionary. There is no calling to be a slave, but only a calling to be a Christian— and to be a Christian while in these states. Paul is not demanding a static society nor forbidding a Christian concern for social changes. Paul would agree that some of these circumstances and states are not optimal and, therefore, they should be changed if possible. But the change is not necessary for one's being a Christian, for his leading the Christian life, his answering his ultimate destiny, his realization of his highest purpose, his accomplishment of the end God has determined for him. In every earthly state and in all earthly conditions a man can fulfill God's demands. Therefore, Paul condemns those who forbid marriage. Marriage in itself is no block to being a Christian and to living the Christian life. God rules the circumstances of the life of each and every man, and each and every man can meet his responsibilities to God in *any* circumstance or state of life.

Beginning at verse 25 Paul applies this principle to the question, "should we marry or remain single," and he concludes that, in so far as a man's *klēsis* is concerned, neither state counts for anything in and of itself. Marriage is not inherently superior to the single state nor vice versa. In certain world conditions [97] and for a person with certain characteristics, [98] the single state is advisable. For other persons under other conditions the married state is to be advocated. Whether one marries or not is not a matter of indifference. It is a question to be decided responsibly on the basis of the givens of each individual case. The decision to marry or to remain single cannot be made simply on the basis of the relative merits of marriage or singleness *per se*. I Corinthians 7 is an example of true Biblical realism. There is in Paul no false, superficial asceticism, which fails to take into account the sexual nature

---

[96] Cf. Gerhard Kittel (ed.), *Theologisches Wörterbuch zum Neuen Testament*, Stuttgart, W. Kohlhammer, 1933–, Vol. 3, pp. 489, 490.

[97] V. 26.

[98] Vs. 8, 9.

of man and its effect upon his spiritual life. Paul will go no further than saying that it is *kalon* for the unmarried and the widows to remain single. [99] He will not command singleness; he only calls it "worthy of recommendation, honorable, praiseworthy, not inferior."

It is the eschatological orientation of Paul that makes it possible for him to say that earthly relationships and conditions are of only relative importance. The concept of the transitory nature and limited significance of marriage and of all other earthly relationships forms the background for his advice in verses 29–31: "from now on, let those who have wives live as though they had none, and those who mourn as though they were not mourning, and those who rejoice as though they were not rejoicing, and those who buy as though they had no goods, and those who deal with the world as though they had no dealings with it. For the form of this world is passing away." The Christian stands in the middle of life, but he is not defined by this earthly life. It does not provide the standard by which he determines what is his purpose in life, what his duties are, what has value,. what is right, what must be rejected. The Christian sees this life as provisional: marrying, buying, selling, mourning, and rejoicing are part of the *schema* of this world, which is passing away. From this background Paul says, "Are you bound to a wife? Do not seek to be free. Are you free from a wife? Do not seek marriage. But if you marry, you do not sin." [100]

There is no universal, absolute obligation to marry, neither for woman nor for man. Man's highest obligation is to serve Christ in the kingdom. He can and must serve Christ in whatever condition, circumstance, and state he lives. Each individual person has his own peculiar relationships and circumstances, [101] and he need not change them in order to realize his ultimate purpose. Paul was no sectarian; he had no fear of pluriformity. Thus, he refused to make an exclusive choice between marriage and singleness: neither is *the* Christian state. In either a person can sin, or he can glorify God.

The solution to the social problem of the older unmarried woman is to be found in changing the standard and ideal of society. A woman is no failure because she has not married. The value of woman is not determined by her marital status. Marriage is not essential to the realization of her ultimate purpose. The presupposition which lies behind society's evaluation and stereotype of the single woman must be rejected without qualification. The church must make known to society her judgment of this presupposition. Only by influencing society to change its ideal can the church exorcise the terror of the "old maid's" existence.

---

[99] V. 8.

[100] Vs. 27, 28a.

[101] Paul's emphasis upon the peculiar circumstances of every individual is pronounced. In each of a series of statements concerning the variety of the Christian life, Paul, by beginning with the word *ekatos,* whether as subject, direct object, or indirect object, emphasizes this individual aspect. Cf. vs. 17, 20, 24.

CHAPTER III

THE PERSONAL PROBLEMS OF THE OLDER UNMARRIED

Acceptance of Singleness

If the older unmarried are to find solutions to the personal problems related to singleness, they must first learn to accept their singleness. Men and women who have worked extensively with the older unmarried as pastors, counselors, and psychotherapists agree that the conscious acceptance of the self as it really is and not as one would like it to be is a prerequisite for solving other personal problems, including the sexual and social problems. John Laurence, a Catholic priest who has counseled older unmarried persons on three continents and has studied their problems for over twenty years, says of the unmarried woman, "The only person who can really help the unwilling celibate is herself." She has to recognize "any behavior, attitude, or rationalization that is an evasion of the truth ... and adjust herself realistically to a world that is ruthless with the dishonest." [1] By characterizing the single woman as "The Reluctant Virgin" [2] he points to this acceptance of singleness— one element in the acceptance of self—as one of her chief problems and to this problem he devotes two chapters, "There Is Folly in Flight" and "The Panic-Stricken and the Defiant." H. Hanselman says a common psychic reaction to singleness is anxiety—and it is rightly named anxiety, for these single persons do not know what it is that they fear, what it is of singleness that disturbs them. They have not yet faced singleness and taken a clear, hard look at what it involves. Until they know the reason for their anxiety they cannot overcome it and until their anxiety is gone, they cannot accept their singleness. [3] Another writer on the problems of singleness counsels the older unmarried that many of them must overcome an obsession with the idea that marriage is a state of perfection. "The commandment 'do not covet' applies here too. Many spoil what could have been a life of outstanding service by spending it all in a 'temporary' vocation. They choose a job as a time-killer until they should marry." [4] From her personal experience and her experience as a pastor J. W. Herfst writes of the unmarried woman, "she must

---

[1] *The Single Woman*, New York, Duell, Sloan, and Pearce, 1952, pp. vi, vii.
[2] *Ibid.*, p. viii.
[3] *Hij en Zij Problemen*, Zeist, Ploegsma, n.d., pp. 191, 192.
[4] Rolf Veenstra, *Christian Marriage*, Hamilton, Guardian Pub. Co., 1957, pp. 43 and 45.

make it clear to herself that also in the unmarried state she has to realize her calling as human being and in that state she bears the full responsibility for her attitude to life and her behavior.... If anyone for whatever reason ... remains unmarried, she must see the consequence clearly and honestly. Singleness means: having *no* husband and *no* children." If the unmarried woman has not accepted her singleness in the full consciousness of what it involves, she has laid herself open for secret affairs and other unworthy substitutes for marriage. [5]

H. R. Wijngaarden names the acceptance of self as the first of the four main problems of adulthood. It is the prerequisite for the acceptance of others (society), the acceptance of the other (love and marriage), and the acceptance of the meaning of life—the other three main problems. The acceptance of self is also the first problem that the adult unmarried person must face and it includes his acceptance of his singleness. Unless the older unmarried person can accept his singleness, his unconscious flight, repression, or overcompensation for this instinctive need of a partner will inhibit his finding true maturity. Only when he has accepted his singleness and what it involves can he accept society and find meaning and sense for his life. [6]

Wijngaarden defines this acceptance of self as the process by which one arrives at social and psychic self-determination, at external and internal independence. The acceptance of self has two parts: the freeing of the self from all infantile, puerile, and adolescent ties and the acceptance of one's own place and calling in life. [7] The person who has accepted his self is no longer determined by his circumstances, instincts, and desires but freely decides through a full recognition of the various forces influencing his decision. Society no longer decides his attitudes and actions for him. Neither is his life determined by his psychic forces. He has achieved a responsible independence through which *he* determines how *he* should live. The responsibility is undiminished. He does not say "*I* decide what *I* want to do" but "*I* decide what is required of *me* in *my* circumstances." [8] To reach this independence a person must learn to be honest with himself and with the world. He must give up all pretence and rationalization. He must let loose all that is untrue and feigned in his self. All rejection of simulation demands the recognition of the emptiness, the un-

---

[5] "De Ongehuwde Vrouw", *Wending*, July/August, 1954, p. 389. The original reads "Maar wel zal zij zich hebben duidelijk te maken, dat zij ook in de ongehuwde staat haar roeping als mens moet verwerkelijken, en daarin de volle verantwoordelijkheid draagt voor haar levenshouding en -gedrag ... Als iemand om welke reden ook ... niet trouwt, zal zij de consequenties eerlijk onder ogen moeten zien. Ongetrouwd-blijven betekent: géén man en géén kinderen hebben." (Translation mine, M. H.).

[6] *Hoofdproblemen der Volwassenheid*, Utrecht, E. J. Bijleveld, 1950, pp. 91–94.

[7] *Ibid.*, pp. 91, 92.

[8] *Ibid.*, p. 106.

importance, and the smallness which this simulation was meant to cover.

Such recognition is the first step to acceptance, but it is not yet acceptance. Having recognized his true self, a person can yet cover it with sham and pretence or use it to awaken sympathy and pity. This latter is an attempt to transfer the responsibility in part or completely to another person or to society generally. [9] He has yet to acknowledge his true self to others and consciously to his own person. Through this self-acknowledgment he accepts the responsibility for his self. Acceptance of self does not mean a lethargic resignation to the status quo. The recognition of what one is and the assumption of full responsibility for the self does not exclude efforts to change: to fill his lacks and emptiness and to satisfy his needs and desires. In so doing a person is not hiding the self or disclaiming responsibility for it, but is being true to his self. Acceptance means recognition and acknowledgment, not resignation. Yet, in his recognition of his calling and place in life he may decide that these desires must remain unsatisfied and his lacks unfilled. Only when a person has discovered and accepted his self as it really is, can he come to the inner preparedness to be neither greater nor smaller nor in any way other than he really is. [10]

Another element in this acceptance of self is the acceptance of life in all its aspects, its sorrows as well as its joys, its failures as well as its successes, its dissatisfactions as well as its satisfactions. The acceptance of the light side of life and of the dark are not unrelated. The man who can genuinely enjoy can also genuinely sorrow. The one ability involves the other for only the man who has accepted his self and thus achieved both psychic and social independence can do either. [11]

Finally, this acceptance of self includes the recognition of one's own value and purpose. The recognition of one's smallness and emptiness and evilness, even that deep recognition which comes through the Christian faith, is not the same as the effacement of self. The Christian faith does not demand the obliteration of self and the denial of its value, but the recognition of the true value and sense of all of God's creation, including that of one's own self. Both inflation of value and deflation, overestimation and underestimation, are excluded by the acceptance of one's true self.

Although this process of acceptance of self begins in puberty, the youth is structurally unable to achieve it. And it is no inevitable step, for some people never acquire this independence, in which they are able responsibly to determine their own lives.

The unmarried face this problem of acceptance of self in no greater measure than the married. The form of their problem, however, will

---

[9] *Ibid.*, pp. 102, 103.
[10] *Ibid.*, p. 106.
[11] *Ibid.*, pp. 107, 108.

differ from that of the married. They will have to recognize and accept different needs and desires and different failures and lacks. For them it is of great importance that they learn to accept their singleness. Not all older unmarried persons have equal difficulty making the mental adjustment to the fact that they are and probably will remain single. The person who remains single because he or she so wished— whether this wish is the result of a responsible decision or a neurotic inhibition—has less trouble accepting his singleness than the person whose singleness was forced upon him by social or personal circumstances.

Laurence writes of the single woman, "If she is forever making excuses for herself, forever pretending, forever explaining, even to people who ask for no explanation, why it is that she never married, then all is not well with her. Occasional feelings of embarrassment are quite in order and are to be expected, but an obstinate, perservering sense of shame is sure evidence of maladjustment." [12] In a society which places a high value upon marriage for a woman and therefore judges the single woman a failure, it is not surprising that the single woman has difficulty recognizing her own value and purpose and in accepting her place and calling in life. And it is no wonder that many women can hardly accept the fact that they can no longer reckon with the possibility of marriage. Laurence describes the case of Maxine, a woman who could not reconcile herself to her unattractiveness and her consequent singleness. For her, singleness was an infirmity which she refused to accept and an insurmountable obstacle to life. She "launched into an indignant condemnation of the abbreviated bikini that was popular on the beaches that summer" because she suspected that she fell short of full womanhood. Her stories of men who had made improper advances to her made it apparent that she was trying to convince herself that men had lusted after her and that she could have been married if she had lowered her standards. Laurence says of her, "I could not help feeling, listening to her, that she would have been consoled, rather than terrified, had a man really assaulted her." [13]

In chapter nine Laurence gives from his experience as a priest several examples of women who have not yet learned to accept their singleness. These examples are included here not because they are exhaustive of the ways a person can react to singleness nor because the method of typing them is necessarily the most fruitful for gaining an insight into their reactions. His descriptions are intentionally more caricatures than characterizations in order to highlight the ways in which a person can flee his singleness and therefore they illustrate the variety of the consequences of this failure.

Laurence divides women who are still embarrassed by their singleness into those who run away from men and those who run after men. The

---

[12]   Op. cit., p. 147.
[13]   Ibid., pp. 123–128.

attitude of the first is a, usually unconscious, "sour grapes" attitude: she convinces herself she does not want the unattainable and she finds something else to take its place. The attitude of the latter is more honest. She recognizes that she does not have what she wants, but she is not willing to leave her want unsatisfied and will pay a high price for its satisfaction.

There are several types of women who flee from men. One Laurence calls "the unbalanced mystic." She is the woman who, because she has failed to attract a man, "seeks solace in the supernatural. God becomes her *lover* in an unwholesome and nauseating mysticism . . . . She does not exist for God, but He for her. She, not God, is the center of her fantastic world." [14] Two other types with which he has come into contact are the "Administrative Fanatic" and the "Simpering Follower." The first is the strong-willed woman who "battles her determined way" to the presidency of the woman's guild, Junior League, or PTA and "becomes a sort of witch doctor determined to smell out the faintest odor of 'sin' . . . . She sets herself up as the unofficial Vice Squad. . . ." The Simpering Follower he describes as the "quiet, docile soul looking for escape from frustration through religion." She either surrenders her own responsibility by meekly following the leadership of others or by "piteous appeals for special guidance" focuses attention upon herself and in this way delegates the responsibility for her own life and her own decisions. [15] The hypochondriac finds meaning and sense in her life through constant attention to her psychic and physical ailments. Her illnesses are her substitute for that unattainable marriage. The "intellectual refugee" seeks to overcome her inferiority feelings and sense of shame over her singleness by scholarly excellence. The "inveterate, incurable joiner" is not merely seeking companionship, but a psychic crutch, a feeling that she is important, that she belongs, that somewhere she is inexpendable. If she is at the same time seeking to call attention to herself, the more eccentric the organization the better it fits her unconscious needs. Laurence makes the comment, somewhat exaggerated but in its intent basically correct: "There is no crack-brained, exotic, esoteric religion that has not somewhere in its inner councils one of the world's fugitive virgins." [16]

Laurence also names various types of women who chase after men. The "aging good-time girl" is the woman who has refused to accept the fact that she is no longer a junior *femme fatale*. She apes the dress and behavior of women years younger, she is proud of her lack of inhibitions, and she loses all sense of decency in her search for a man. Other women show their neurotic eagerness for male companionship in other ways. Some greet every man as a starving person would a chanced-

---

[14] *Ibid.*, p. 148.
[15] *Ibid.*, pp. 148–150.
[16] *Ibid.*, p. 152.

upon piece of bread. This indiscreet eagerness may frighten away the man or it may make these women prey to the libertine Casanova. The "Kept Woman" has "more regard for her pride . . . and wants her friendship on a more permanent basis," but she too is trying to solve the problem of her singleness by finding a man outside of marriage if she cannot have him in marriage. [17]

Not all these types are necessarily single. A woman may have similar reactions to an unsatisfactory marriage. Nor are these types all necessarily feminine. In so far as a man regards his singleness a lack and a failure, he is vulnerable to similar rationalizations and pretence. Since, however, society generally regards singleness as an advantage for the male, there is less likelihood that he will have serious difficulty accepting it.

Secondly, besides accepting the fact that they are and may well remain single the older unmarried in their acceptance of self must learn to accept their sexuality and what singleness means for it. They must recognize their sexual desires and acknowledge them to themselves. Unless they do this, their repressed sexual desires will prevent them from achieving the psychic and social independence necessary for the genuine acceptance of others, for their attitudes and decisions will never be fully free but always in part forced by unconscious motivations. This acceptance of sexuality has three elements for the older unmarried. First they must recognize and acknowledge their sexual drive and desires. There is a rare possibility that the person who says "I never have such desires" is telling the truth, but in all probability these desires are only unrecognized by the conscious mind. Such repression is dangerous because it keeps the desire unconscious and therefore largely outside the control of the person. He does not control the desire. It controls him. The removal of such repressions in some cases demands the service of a psychotherapist. Secondly, the older unmarried must realize that their sexual desires and drives are good, not evil or sinful. They must understand that their sexual arousal by another person, a thought, or a situation is never wrong because it is sexual. This desire is a legitimate desire. But finally they must accept the fact that the desire must remain unsatisfied as long as they are not joined to another in marriage. This conscious, considered, genuine acknowledgment is the *sine qua non* for the solution to their personal sexual problems. Although an unsolved conflict may lie relatively dormant for many years, any strong emotional shock, even though it is seemingly unrelated to the original conflict, may set it off. These unsolved sexual problems become especially urgent for both men and women in the period of the climacteric, or change of life. A heightened sexual sensitivity and strong sexual desires, common to this period, combined with weakened inhibitions brought on by mental depression and feelings of loneliness, also common in the

---

[17] *Ibid.*, pp. 154–156.

climateric, [18] can have disastrous effects for the single person who has not learned to accept his sexuality. The influence of the acceptance of one's sexuality upon particular sexual problems will be discussed in more detail later.

For many unmarried women and possibly some unmarried men the unsatisfied desire for a child is an aspect of singleness that is one of the most difficult to accept. "The mere fact of going without mating, physical and mental, of not having that natural satisfaction which is sought by almost all living creatures is, of course, the deepest and the most unmanageable," writes Margery Fry. "But in many women the desire for children is an instinct at least as profound as that of sex." [19]

Not all women feel the desire for a child equally. In some women this desire seems to be absent. In others it is not strong enough to inhibit their acceptance of singleness. For some unmarried women, however, it is one of their chief problems. Part of this problem is not, strictly speaking, a maternal desire for a child. The desire for companionship, to have someone to love and to care for and to have someone who loves

---

[18] O. van Andel Ripke, *De Moeilijkste Jaren*, Utrecht, E. J. Bijleveld, 1952, p. 100. For the psychic reactions common to the female climacteric see Helene Deutsch, *The Psychology of Women*, London, Research Books, 1947, Vol. 2, pp. 402, 403, and B. Chr. Hamer, *Zielzorg en Psychiatrie*, Kampen, J. H. Kok, 1952, pp. 114–116. For the psychic reactions found in the male climacteric see Kenneth Walker, "Sex in Middle Age," *Sex in Social Life*, S. Neville-Rolfe (ed.), London, Allen and Unwin, 1949, pp. 435–439.

[19] *The Single Woman*, London, Delisle, 1953, pp. 8, 9. While Fry's statement of the strength of this desire is accurate her naming it an "instinct" is misleading. On p. 11 she defines this "instinct" as the instinctive urge "to mate and produce offspring, which man shares with animals." This statement is scientifically inaccurate, for neither man nor animal has an instinct to produce offspring, only a sex drive which demands physical satisfaction, as the result of which reproduction occurs. There are still human societies which deny altogether a causal connection between sexual intercourse and conception and in nearly all societies there are shielded women who do not learn how children are conceived until after they are pregnant. The sex act is not the results of a "procreative instinct." Once the relation between sexual intercourse and reproduction has been learned, part of the motivation for sexual intercourse may be a desire for children, but what must be learned can hardly be called an instinct. As A. Kardiner says, the primary object of sexual activity is orgastic pleasure. All other goals or purposes are learned. *Sex and Morality*, New York, Bobbs-Merril, 1954, p. 170.

The accuracy of the term "maternal instinct" is also being questioned. Helene Deutsch says, "At present it is difficult to decide to what extent the complex emotional attribute that we call 'motherliness' expresses a biologic condition," *The Psychology of Women*, Vol. 2, p. 12. Weatherhead would rather call it an inclination than an instinct, *Psychologie ten Dienste van de Ziel*, Utrecht, E. J. Bijleveld, 1940, p. 210. Psychologists generally agree that the so-called "maternal instinct" is in a large measure a cultural product. Whether it has a biologic basis or not, and if so, to what extent, need not concern us here because it remains true that the average 20th century woman of Western civilization deeply desires a child to raise and care for and she is psychically fitted for the task. This desire, whether instinctive or culturally produced, must be considered in this thesis since many single women find this unsatisfied desire one of the most troubling problems of their singleness.

them and needs them, is fused with what Deutsch calls the "will to motherhood" [20] so that they become identified in the single woman's mind. Were the desire for companionship and love abated, what she experiences as a desire for a child would also lessen.

Fry describes the single woman's deep desire for a child by quoting a rather sentimental but nevertheless enlightening poem entitled "Old Maid's Child."

> Child of my body whom I never bore
> Dear fruit of all a woman's fruitless pain
> Come, nestle in these empty arms again,
> Come, nuzzle at my milkless breast once more.
>
> You cannot feel, and yet I hear your cries.
> You seem to weep because, since you are blind,
> You cannot even see if I am kind.
> Hush, darling! look through other children's eyes. [21]

This imaginative realization of an unconceived and unborn child is not only a literary device. It is a psychic possibility. Some single women and childless married women derive much comfort from a carefully formed mental image of the child they did not have. This child has a certain reality for them although this reality is only in their imagination and they realize that this is so. Fry refers to this phenomenon, though rather facetiously: "Old maid's children are proverbially perfect, and it appears that they inherit this characteristic from their imagined fathers." [22] The existence of an imaginary child need not have become as real as a delusion to affect her ability to accept others and to give herself to others. In so far as this "child she didn't have" occupies her attention and thoughts, she is living in a dream world divorced from reality. It holds her back from a personal acceptance of her position and calling in life.

Even without indulgence in fantasy the unrecognized and unacknowledged desire for a child can hold a woman back from psychic independence. Unconsciously her choice of vocation may be determined not by a recognition of what life demands of her with her abilities and in her situation but by her unconscious, unsatisfied desire for a child. A strong maternal desire may have a furthering influence in the practice of several professions, such as teaching, nursing, and social work. It may also have a disturbing effect, especially if the desire and its satisfaction are unconscious. Many otherwise "efficient women... constantly fall into conflicts because of their inability to master their

---

20   *Op. cit.*, p. 21.
21   *Op. cit.*, p. 9. No credit given.
22   *Ibid.*, pp. 17, 18.

hostile feelings toward the mothers of their charges." [23] These women may be totally unaware of the psychic motivation for these conflicts. They may feel that the conflict stems, for example, from the mothers' reactionary opposition to practices of proven scientific value, when actually these childless women are using these practices to give vent to their unconscious feelings of jealousy. These women have not yet mastered their desire for a child. It is controlling them. The first step for control of the desire is conscious recognition and acknowledgment of the desire. They must accept also this aspect of singleness: singleness means having no child.

The failure to accept childlessness is the source of emotional disturbances, especially in the climacteric. Unmarried women have approximately the same amount and type of physical symptoms and disturbances in this period as married women, [24] but psychic disturbances such as irritability, nervous apprehension, and depression are more common for the unmarried woman. This nervous instability is usually related to their being alone, their facing old age, and their not having children. [25] The menopause, the cessation of those physical processes which enable them to bear children, means the end of all hopes of someday having a child. It is this finality which disturbs single women if they have not yet accepted their childlessness. For example, single women in this period are often jealous of younger women, especially young married women. They feel that their jealousy is wrong and an unconscious struggle with their conscience results. This struggle is often expressed in self-blame as "I have never been of any use to anyone" or "I always do everything wrong." [26] These self-accusations and the underlying guilt feelings and jealousy cannot be overcome until the single woman has learned to accept her childlessness.

Deutsch illustrates this intensified desire for a child in the climacteric with the story of a fifty year old single woman who had led a "peaceful, contented existence for many years and who had become attached to her work. One day, while dining with friends, she heard that another employed woman was about to give birth to a child, and would be glad to take someone into her home as a mother substitute. The old spinster was asked facetiously whether she would accept this job. She laughed, but from that moment on the idea did not leave her head; she was as though obsessed by the prospect of having a child. She left her good position and sacrificed all the rest of her life to this child of another woman." Deutsch adds, however, that this is not the usual reaction to the recently aroused latent desire for children: "in most

---

[23] *Deutsch,* op. cit., Vol. 2, p. 27.

[24] Laura Hutton refers to a medical investigation of over one thousand women which concluded that single women were slightly more free of physical disturbances than the married. See *Sex in Social Life,* S. Neville-Rolfe (ed.), p. 443.

[25] *Ibid.*

[26] van Andel-Ripke, *op. cit.,* p. 66.

cases, old spinsters and childless women, when it is too late to make up for their missed motherhood, and the psychologic reaction is that of 'sour grapes', become intolerant and impatient toward children, who pay them back with spiteful hate." [27]

The menopause can have a liberating effect upon the single woman who has been dominated by her desire to have a child. "Especially unmarried or childless women who in their eternal hope that 'it may still happen' have been unable to devote themselves wholeheartedly to other things, are as though newborn after ... they have been deprived of their last chance of motherhood. They free their vital energies from the immobility of waiting and put them to use in productive occupations." [28] This liberation comes not from the menopause itself, but from the woman's acceptance of her childlessness when menopause comes. Should she fail to accept it even then, her productive ability will not be bettered.

Singleness does not demand the rejection of all satisfaction of the desire for a child. There are many ways in which the single person can find legitimate satisfaction for this desire through his or her profession, family relationships, and leadership and supervision of children and youth groups in the church and community. Otto Piper distinguishes four elements in the longing for children, of which all except the first can be satisfied outside the parent-child relationship: a sexual element, the desire to physically care for and fondle children, the desire to form a new character and person, and finally, the desire to continue in the stream of history through their children. [29] One of the great benefits of this desire is that it can be a strong force calling them out of their isolation and into communion with other persons, having different personalities, from other milieus, and of other generations.

But even the use of these means of satisfaction demands the acceptance of the limitations of singleness. Seldom, if ever, can unmarried persons find complete satisfaction of this desire, for the awareness that the children for whom they care are never their children in the same sense that a child is his parent's always inhibits it. Secondly, they must accept their singleness because true communion demands the ability to give oneself to another. As long as their contact with children is primarily a means for satisfaction of self, in this case the self's desire for a child, they are failing to establish the genuine communion so important for them as single persons. Only through their aceptance of singleness as meaning also having no child of their own can they accept the child as he is, the child of other parents, and not as they would have him, their own child.

---

27   Op. cit., Vol. 2, p. 425.

28   Deutsch, op. cit., Vol. 2, p. 406.

29   Het Geslachtsleven, Zijn Betekenis en Zijn Geheim, Utrecht, E. J. Bijleveld, 1937, p. 43. See also Piper's The Christian Interpretation of Sex, New York, Scribners, 1955, pp. 47–49.

The acceptance of self, as described above, is necessary also for a person's response to God. In this respect, a person's dedication of his self to God is similar to the dedication to any other person or ideal. The difference between true and false religion does not lie here. Until a person has recognized and acknowledged his self as it really is, until he has accepted his place and calling in life, he cannot fully give himself. This psychological law holds as well for the Christian in his dedication to God as for the Communist in his dedication to the State. Both the result of this dedication and the value of the result are determined not by the nature of the act of dedication but by the object of the dedication. The words of Jesus "For whoever would save his life will lose it: and whoever loses his life for my sake will find it" [30] express not simply a psychological law of the necessity of giving the self but emphasize the supreme importance of the object of this dedication, "for my sake." This does not, however, change the fact that the only man who can fully give himself is the man who knows the self he gives. [31]

The older unmarried as well as every other person must learn to say with Paul that it is not marriage or singleness, slavery or freedom, circumcision or uncircumcision that is of supreme importance, but the serving of God in these states. [32] The statement of Paul to the Philippians "I have learned, in whatever state I am, to be content" [33] expresses this acceptance of one's position and calling in life. It is not the apathetic expression of an inert or discouraged man but the deeply religious expression of a man who had abandoned all personal ambition and desire in complete dedication to the risen Lord. This is a man who has truly accepted his self. Only that man can say "Yes, Lord" to the command "Whatever your hand finds to do, do it with your might." [34]

Aloneness

Aloneness has been called the fundamental problem of the older unmarried. [35] And perhaps it is, for the distinction of most, if not all, of their personal problems can be traced to their isolation. The sex drive is a problem because they are isolated from that male-female relationship of marriage. The motivation for extramarital affairs is in part the search for companionship. Social isolation has a strong influence upon the desire to masturbate. Approaching old age is particularly threatening because they are alone, companionless, unattended. Their spiritual problems are intensified by their social isolation, for they miss much of that communion of believers which is necessary for the building up

---

[30] Matt. 16 : 25, Mark. 8 : 35, and Luke 9 : 24.
[31] Wijngaarden, *Hoofdproblemen*, pp. 113—117.
[32] I Cor. 7 : 17—24.
[33] Phil. 4 : 11.
[34] Eccles. 9 : 10.
[35] Laura Hutton, *De Ongehuwde Vrouw*, Amsterdam, Andries Blitz, n.d., p. 13.

of faith and love. They commonly feel a lack of purpose and sense to life—a religious problem—because of their detachment from society.

Personal isolation is not peculiar to the older unmarried. The urbanization of modern society has concentrated the population as never before. Rapid means of transportation and communication have almost made complete isolation an impossibility. There are few places left where a man can be literally alone for any extended period of time. Today men have more contact with others than in any other period of world history. Americans want and need extensive social contact. American society has woven into its structure a sense of the high value of companionship and social intercourse. Margaret Mead says, " . . . we are a gregarious people, needing the presence of others to give us a full sense of ourselves." [36] Although Americans fear isolation and do much to avoid it, T. S. Eliot has correctly analyzed Western civilization when in *The Cocktail Party* he points out that modern man is separated from his fellow by a deep cleft. As in a prison, each lives next to the other but no one can see his fellow. Each is alone to himself. Modern man lives out of and for himself in a way unknown in a previous age which had a broadly inclusive hierarchical form of the family, in which the home was the unit of industry, and in which the village and church formed one's social frame of reference. This personal isolation is a by-product of the individualization of consciousness in our culture. The native who lives and thinks and reacts and decides communally, not as an individual part of his society but as an extension of the one whole, the tribe, never experiences the aloneness of modern man. The individualization of consciousness has brought many benefits, but it is not unmitigated progress.

Some relationships in modern society afford signal opportunities for genuine personal communion, for overcoming personal isolation, for the creation of an I-Thou relationship, for psychic and spiritual dialogue. Those most commonly providing such opportunity are the marriage relationship of a man and woman and the parent-child relationship. Both of these are part of the family. The family is one of the last holdouts against the individualization process of Western civilization in which the basic unit of society is regarded as the solitary person and not any organic group of persons. The first of these relationships is not for the older unmarried and the second is of little value for them since they have only the child role, never the role of parent. As they grow older, this relationship no longer keeps them within the family and protects them from isolation. The word "family" has come to mean fewer and fewer people. The boundaries of the home have been narrowed down by excluding from it the grandmother, the unmarried sister or brother, and the unmarried daughter or son. "Family" now means the biological family consisting of a husband, a wife, and young

---

[36]   *Male and Female*, London, Victor Gollancz, 1949, p. 328.

or no children. [37] This limitation means two things: the unmarried person cannot live in the home of his parents or brother or sister, and also these cannot live in the home of the unmarried person. Married couples are expected to be self-sufficient, even in old age. They cannot look forward to homes with their children or siblings, not even the unmarried ones. Margaret Mead has summed up this social attitude: most Americans feel that in all forms of household other that that of the biological family "somebody will be ... sacrificed to somebody else. ... Unmarried children who are self-supporting shouldn't be clinging to the home; they should get out and get married and start homes of their own;" and if they cannot or will not get married, they should at least get out. [38]

The breakdown of family clan-living has exerted social pressure upon the older unmarried to find his or her dwelling apart from the members of the family and other developments have made it possible to do so. Women today are an accepted part of the working force in nearly every field of activity. The unmarried woman seldom has to depend upon the support of parents or siblings. She can support herself and create her own life with her own home. Nor is there any stigma attached to a woman's working. Society approves her efforts at self-support. Secondly, America has a high standard of living with correspondingly high wages, which makes it possible for a working single man or woman to live alone and live well. The level of employment is high enough to provide work for the single woman as well as the single man.

There are other concomitant social factors which intensify the aloneness of the older unmarried. The urbanization of America and the mobility of American people results in a migration of large numbers of people from the communities in which they were born and grew up. The older unmarried, too, often move to other areas, seeking satisfactory employment and a freer life. In moving they often increase their aloneness by leaving friends, acquaintances, and relatives. The social attitude toward the older unmarried woman drives many farther into social isolation. Society does not welcome the presence and friendship of the single woman in the same way it does that of the single man. Part of the isolation comes from the single woman herself. She tends to withdraw from society because of inferiority feelings which are the result of the social attitude. These social factors, which tend to exclude the older unmarried from the family and intimate social relationships, have made their aloneness more real and more intense than in other ages and other cultures.

Aloneness is not the same as loneliness. Loneliness is an emotional dejection which comes from personal isolation. The physical isolation of a person in a desert or in a lifeboat on the ocean may cause loneliness

---

[37] *Ibid.*, pp. 325, 326.
[38] *Ibid.*

but not necessarily. Also, such physical isolation is not a necessary factor in loneliness, for a man can be lonely in a crowd. Any lack of personal communion through the creation of an I-Thou relationship can cause loneliness, even though there is extensive contact on more superficial levels. This lack of regular contact on a personal level characterizes the situation of the older unmarried. They may or may not be lonely, but they are alone in a way that a person who is part of a family living-unit as husband, wife, or minor child is not. And loneliness is not the only possible result of aloneness. Little work has as yet been done on the psychic and spiritual effects of isolation. Such work is just now beginning in preparation for coming space travel, manned weather stations in the Arctic, nuclear submarine warfare, etc. These experiments study a social isolation which is more severe than that of the older unmarried and which has other modifying factors as a limited area of activity and the monotony of a limited number of psychic stimuli, but such studies will give much information on the effects of isolation which will be valuable for understanding the aloneness of the older unmarried, for there is similarity as well as difference in their situations.

This aloneness of the older unmarried can perhaps best be described by considering the nature of those particular communions [39] which occur in marriage and the family and which the single person either misses completely or must seek in other relationships. Marriage is not the only relationship in which these several kinds of communion can be had, nor is it necessarily the most fruitful relationship for the production of these communions, but it has this particular value, it is for most people an inescapable, sustained opportunity for the creation of such communions within a social form that is approved by society. Such communions are only opportunities in marriage, not necessary consequences of it. Many married persons fail to achieve such communions and suffer psychic and spiritual inhibitions equivalent to those of many unmarried. Yet the situation of the two differs, for the older unmarried have no such inescapable, sustained opportunity. They must exert themselves to create relationships in which these communions can be had and therefore many never acquire them. Another inhibiting factor is that often nearly the only social forms in which such a communion is possible or probable are social forms of which society tacitly or explicitly disapproves. For example, the personal communion of two sexes is acquired with difficulty by the older unmarried person because a close, personal relationship

---

[39]   The word "communion" is used here in the literal sense of "a union with," "a comm-union." Essential to this communion is genuine communication, a mutual exchange, dialogue in the sense in which the newer psychologies use the term. This communication is not necessarily conscious or verbal. A person communicates with another by his reactions to events, situations, and things with which the other person is not involved. Two people living together communicate by their whole lives. Another modern term used by both psychology and theology to designate this communion is "encounter."

with either a married or an unmarried person of the other sex is usually *per se* suspect. Finally, marriage and the family under normal circumstances provide regular, extensive contact on a personal level. The mere fact that the family forms a living unit is one of its more important benefits. The husband-wife and child-parent contact occurs daily over a long period of time. The personal contact of the older unmarried is often, by comparison, irregular and less extensive and therefore affords much less opportunity for genuine communion. Also, much of the contact of the older unmarried is on the impersonal level. They may have more of this kind of contact, but it does little to overcome their aloneness. For example, in a business contact two people approach each other primarily as representatives of their firm or their department within the firm. Their contact is not subjective, but objective. Their personalities, their personal problems, and their aspirations and needs are either intentionally excluded from consideration or are made subservient to the business to be accomplished.

Marriage is, first of all, a communion of two individuals. Two persons are joined together in such a way that they become a unity in which each regards the other as his own self, caring for the other and desiring the other's welfare, comforting the other, warning the other, supporting the other, encouraging the other, loving the other. The relationship of parent and child has something of this character, but marriage is the lifelong, exclusive relationship of two mature persons. This communion is not necessarily conscious or verbal. The woman who cares for her home and prepares dinner for her husband when he comes from work and the man who works five days a week for the support of his family are expressing this unity in a communion through service of the other.

Communion between individuals is necessary for a person's psychic and spiritual well-being. The common stereotype of the egocentric single man or single woman is not wholly without basis in fact. Fry names as one of the possible effects of isolation the narrowing of one's world to that with which the self is immediately concerned. "The person who lives too much alone is apt to . . . [lay too] much stress on things of small importance. The little world, the daily habits, the precious belongings, must not be tampered with—a spot of ink on the carpet, or the milkman's calling late will ruin the whole day." [40] The over-fastidious single woman, who sees each stray bit of lint as a threat to her existence; the hypochondriac, who regards every twinge and bodily process as a symptom of illness; the miserly single man or woman, who collects old newspapers, old furniture, and odds and ends, unable to throw away anything that he or she might later need; and the person to whom reality has no worth or meaning except in so far as it is his own—all these lack communion. They have never become engaged in society. They lack genuine communication with others. They are

---

[40] *Op. cit.*, pp. 25, 26.

shut off, isolated and therefore their life revolves around themselves and their own. The embittered, sour single person, who either withdraws from society as a recluse or attacks society wherever it touches his or her life, has also failed to achieve communion. [41]

Lack of communion is not traceable simply to a failure to give the self, a failure to love, a failure to respond in this dialogue of persons. It takes two to make a communion and to communicate. The well-known anecdote of the lonely little orphan girl tells only half the story. Daily she walked out into the woods, stayed a few moments, and then returned. The matron became curious and followed her one day to find that the little girl was walking out every day to see if anyone had taken the small note she had left on a tree. It read, "Whoever finds this, I love you." But the little girl also meant, "Whoever finds this, please love me." Man needs not only to love but also to be loved. He needs not only some one to be concerned about, but someone to be concerned about him. Without this concern of another, life loses much of its meaning and purpose. As one single woman stated it, ". . . one of the stings of singleness is just that you have to bear it alone. . . ." [42] Karen Horney names as one of the chief psychic principles which give power to instincts, urges, and needs, the safety principle. Man seeks safety not only in the physical sense but also in the psychic sense. He needs to feel secure from those things which threaten his psychic existence. "People can renounce food, money, attention, affection so long as they are only renouncing satisfaction, but they cannot renounce these things if without them they would be or feel in danger of destitution or starvation or of being helplessly exposed to hostility, in other words, if they would lose their feeling of safety." Then Horney singles out isolation as one of the environmental forces which instills this anxiety over one's security and leads to psychic disturbances and eccentricity. [43] Isolation has this effect whether it is self-imposed or imposed by others. The single woman, for example, may be ready to join society as an active member but if society refuses to accept her because of the stereotyped judgment of the unmarried woman, she may, through her isolation, become what society thinks she is. The mere presence of another person and the opportunity to talk about fears, needs, or desires lessen their force, even when the other person is powerless to overcome or satisfy them. The so-called "moral support" of another person is beneficial to psychic well-being. Even more, personal communion is

---

[41] "Die Isolierung nahm zu, die die Frauen fühlten sich einsam und verlassen, enttäuscht. Sie wussten mit sich und mit dem Leben nichts mehr anzufangen, und die Folge war im allgemeinen eine mehr oder minder grosse Verbitterung, eine Unzufriedenheit, ein stiller Vorwurf gegen ihre Umgebung, der sie bei dieser nicht gerade beliebter machte." Erich Stern, *Die Unverheirateten*, Stuttgart, Ferdinand Enke, 1957, p. 9.

[42] Fry, *op. cit.*, p. 8.

[43] *New Ways in Psychoanalysis*, London, Routledge and Kegan Paul, 1954, pp. 73 and 75.

necessary for psychic and spiritual welfare. In isolation a person's fears, needs, and desires assume overwhelming proportions. The author of Ecclesiastes recognized this human need of the support of another: "Two are better than one, because they have a good reward for their toil. For if they fall, one will lift up his fellow; but woe to him who is alone when he falls and has not another to lift him up. Again, if two lie together, they are warm; but how can one be warm alone?" [44]

Marriage is also, as W. F. Teeuwen points out, [45] a communion of two personalities with two viewpoints and from two milieus. Marriage gives a person the opportunity to see, understand, and compare another milieu and viewpoint. The isolated man or woman is always in danger of becoming static because no relationship forces him or her to consider other possibilities. There are various forms of static personalities: the dogmatic person whose convictions are not subject to change, the fanatic whose life is ruled by one idea, the psychically impoverished person who finds life dull and whom other people find dull because he has little or no interest in anything different or new, and the unsympathetic person who cannot understand anyone with a different personality and character from his own. These people have failed to grow, change, and mature. Their staticism is not just a psychic problem. The inflexible person does not suddenly become flexible in his religious life. All these forms of staticism are evident also in the various personal responses to the gospel. Their static personalities tend to inhibit their full salvation. The dogmatic person finds it hard to grow in faith and knowledge of his Lord Jesus Christ. The fanatic finds it hard to appreciate all the aspects of the gospel because for him the one element blocks out all the rest. The psychically impoverished person and the unsympathetic person can hardly become all things to all men that they might by all means save some because for the former an interest in the problems of others is lacking and for the latter the necessary adaptability.

Thirdly, in marriage two or more age groups come into communion. Nearly all persons, married or unmarried have some contact and communion with the previous generation, that of their parents. In marriage and the resulting family, contact with the succeeding generations creates the opportunity for communion. Again, the particular value of marriage is that it usually gives inescapable, regular, sustained contact, plus strong motives for creating communion. Communion with persons of other age groups is acquired with difficulty. Youth experiences its own existence as an encounter with all that exists and everything that happens. All is his business because it is all part of his existence. Therefore he is ready to call anything and everything into question and it is all subject to discussion. But dialogue,

---

[44] Eccles. 4 : 9—11.
[45] "Op Huwelijksvoorwaarde," *Man en Vader,* Zwolle, La Rivière and Voorhoeve, 1953, G. Lugtigheid (ed.), p. 14.

discussion, communion, with the older generation is difficult because for them it is important that a number of these questions are placed outside of discussion. Their life has meaning and sense because some things are fixed and certain. The youth, however, feels that this refusal to call certain things into question is an attack upon his complete existence. [46] This is the phenomena meant when youth is called, rather inaccurately, radical and older people conservative. This and other differences between the youth and his elders is the source of much misunderstanding and friction. Within the love relationship of the family there is the opportunity for understanding and communion. Here lies the element of truth in the statement "You cannot understand children until you have a child of your own." This is also one of the reasons why some church councils hesitate to nominate unmarried persons for an office in the church.

Also, the youth are a part of the present age in a way that an older person can never be. The older person is always qualified by his past. He has been formed by his past experiences and by past eras. He is still being formed, but these new influences always have givens formed in the past to work upon. The child and the youth are by comparison virgin territory. Another difference is that the older person is oriented more to his past. He reflects upon his past and upon the meaning of life [47] and tends to interpret the present in terms of related phenomena in his past. Contact and communion with the younger generations helps the older generation retain the flexibility necessary for an understanding of modern times, of modern problems, and of modern solutions.

Fourthly, marriage is a communion of two sexes. Regardless of whether the non-anatomical differences of man and woman are innate or acquired, these differences do exist. Many attempts have been made to define these differences and to account for them. Two of the better known studies are that of Havelock Ellis, *Man and Woman*, [48] and of L. M. Terman and C. C. Miles, *Sex and Personality: Studies in Masculinity and Femininity*. [49] Both point to certain interests, abilities, values, types of emotional reactions, and characteristics that are found more generally or more pronouncedly in the one sex or the other. Psychologists agree that there is no rigid sexual division of personality traits or characteristics and that one can only speak of a masculine or feminine personality in a relative sense since there is a wide range of individual variation and a considerable area of overlapping. Yet there are general psychic differences between men and women. Through the communion between the two sexes in marriage and in the social life of married people, these values and characteristics of the other sex are known and appreciated. The man or woman who has not learned

---

[46]   Waterink, "Jeugdproblemen," *Centrale Weekblad*, July 4, 1953, p. 145.

[47]   Wijngaarden, *Hoofdproblemen*, pp. 234–246.

[48]   Eighth edition revised, London, W. Heinemann, 1934.

[49]   New York, McGraw-Hill, 1936.

to know and appreciate the value of the psychic traits characteristic of the other sex, is the person who has failed to establish communion with that sex. In the older unmarried this failure can often be traced to a lack of personal, regular, and sustained contact with the other sex. The contact they have may be generally impersonal. A personal approach to either a married or an unmarried person of the other sex is often misconstrued as something other than a desire for friendship. This isolation from the other sex is an isolation from the tempering, balancing influence of that sex. As a result both the isolated man and the isolated woman can become extreme embodiments of the characteristics of their sex. If that which characterizes femininity can be summarized, as does F. J. J. Buytendijk, [50] as "het verzorgen"—that is, woman lives out of an intentional consciousness of the concrete presence of persons and things, whose value is discovered, protected, and magnified by her personal participation and care—then that type of single woman who fusses over her home, her clothes, her nieces and nephews, her garden or her art, her literature, her social work, or even her religious faith, is at least partially explained. It is not so much that she takes care of that which she loves, as she loves that which she takes care of. That very valuable feminine characteristic which is so important for motherhood and homemaking has not been tempered by the masculine approach of life, which Buytendijk calls "het arbeiden": that is, living and acting more out of a consciousness of preconceived goals which are independent from the actions themselves, seeing the world more as a system of means to reach those goals, and not accepting it only for its own inherent value; thus living more autonomously, prospectively, directed to the distant, and expansively. [51] This one-sided emphasis upon the feminine side of her personality is not the only possible reaction to the isolation from the other sex. Wijngaarden enumerates three others. Again using the example of the single woman, although these reactions are equally possible for the single man—she may suppress the feminine side of her personality and develop the masculine aspects of her nature. Sometimes a woman is successful in this attempt and becomes, for example, the detached scientist or the business executive. Or she may so desire the contact between the sexes that she uses her sexual and erotic attractiveness to form contact on these levels. Our culture contains strong motivations to choose this reaction since the sexual contact between man and woman is so highly valued. Though this woman may, whenever she meets a man, embark upon a campaign of flirtation and sexual teasing and may even have repeated sexual affairs, the deeper motivation for her actions is not sexual. This motivation will be discussed at greater length when the sexual problems of the older unmarried are analyzed. A third

---

[50]   *De Vrouw*, Utrecht, Het Spectrum, 1951, pp. 290, 291.
[51]   *Ibid.*, p. 290.

possible reaction is disappointment, antagonism, and self-pity. This person may direct her antagonism to society generally and become a bitter recluse. Her antagonism may also be directed to one sex: to men because she feels that they have rejected her, or to women, including herself, because she feels that femininity has betrayed her. It has not given that which it promised. [52] These reactions are not mutually exclusive. A woman may, for example, become a man-hater and have a one-sided development of the feminine side of her personality. Nor are these types necessary consequences of isolation from the other sex. They are only possible reactions. As Wijngaarden points out, the single woman can also join battle with those forces in society which isolate her and seek to develop and use new social forms and customs. [53]

The same can be true of the isolated man. He can become an extreme embodiment of that which characterizes his sex. The man who fails to establish communion with women can become completely absorbed in his occupation and his efforts to achieve his goals. All reality which is not involved in these efforts fades out of his life. Therefore, the picture of the absent-minded professor and that of the preoccupied scientist are nearly always of men. His relationship to other people, to their problems and trials, to their needs and desires is neither recognized nor considered. Or he can become a misanthrope, a misogynist, or a sexual Don Juan.

Other psychologists define the masculine-feminine difference in 20th century Western civilization somewhat differently and use different terms to describe it, [54] but whatever the difference, they agree that for full psychic development one needs communion with the other sex.

Finally, marriage is a communion in faith. As W. F. Teeuwen expresses it, for the Christian, marriage is ultimately "een werkgemeen-schap in Christus' Rijk," a work-communion in Christ's kingdom. [55] Man and woman are joined together to serve God, to submit to his rule, and to raise their children in the fear and nurture of the Lord. Such a communion of faith as exists in the Christian marriage is of very great value for growth in faith and love, for the overcoming of religious doubt, and for resistance against temptation. This communion of faith is that *koinonia* which plays such a significant role in the life and concepts of the New Testament church. The influence of this *koinonia* upon the faith and life of the believer goes beyond that of ordinary social pressure, the social demand for conformity. It is a social pressure, but one which rises out of an intimate communion which is established by their common communion with Christ. [56] This fellowship

---

[52]   *Gesprekken met Uzelf*, Utrecht, E. J. Bijleveld, 1955, p. 177.

[53]   *Ibid.*

[54]   M. E. Harding, for example, characterizes the masculine psyche as Logos and the feminine as Eros, *The Way of All Women*, p. 282.

[55]   *Op. cit.*, p. 20.

[56]   "That which we have seen and heard we proclaim also to you, so that you

is one which has a religious basis and a religious purpose. It is one of the means used by God to bring man to full salvation, as well as being one of the fruits of salvation. [57] Marriage is not, or course, the only place in which this fellowship can be had, but it gives choice opportunity for it. The unmarried person must often create the contact necessary for such communion. For example, the person who is a member of a large metropolitan church in which few people know or have any personal contact with the people sitting next to them in the pew seldom achieves such extensive communion in faith as is found between a Christian man and wife.

When a person fails to achieve the various types of communion named above, the most common psychic consequence is loneliness. The emotional dejection of loneliness is often accompanied by the feeling that one's life has no sense or value. Often the deeper the dejection of loneliness, the deeper is this feeling. Singleness is by no means the only situation which is conducive to loneliness. J. H. Gunning in *Een-zaamheid* [58] lists some sixty different situations and conditions which are often the occasion of loneliness. All these are conditions or situations in which the person has insufficient communion of one type or the other. The older unmarried have these situations and conditions in common with all other people, but by being single they miss also the marriage communions of two individuals, of two milieus, of two or more generations, of two sexes, and of two believers. The emotional dejection of loneliness may be a reaction to insufficient communion of any one or all of these types. The unmarried man who has bachelor friends is not, therefore, immune to loneliness, for his communion with them does not include the communion with the other sex or with succeeding generations.

It has been suggested that religious faith, communion with God, is *the* cure for loneliness. [59] The man who can say with full conviction, "I am known of God" and "in body and soul, in life and in death I am not my own but belong to my Lord and Savior Jesus Christ" and "I am sure that neither death, nor life, nor angels, nor principalities, nor things present, nor things to come, ... nor anything else in creation will be able to separate us from the love of God in Christ Jesus our Lord" has a communion and a fellowship that will protect him from much loneliness. This communion gives sense and purpose to life and brings with it an awareness of one's own value before God. This faith must be a true faith, rooted in a genuine inner conviction. Hutton warns

---

may have fellowship with us; and our fellowship is with the Father and with his son Jesus Christ," I John 1 : 3.

[57] See Acts 2 : 42—fellowship is named with the teaching of the apostles, the breaking of bread, and praying as one of the activities to which the newly baptized believers devoted themselves.

[58] Leiden, "Pniël," 1936.

[59] Gunning, *op. cit.*, p. 50.

that otherwise it can be an escape measure, a neurotic expression. It can be the daydreams of a woman who wishes to be a child, an expression of obsessive, exaggerated guilt and inferiority feelings, or an answer to infantile demands for love and attention, resulting in a sentimental and pathological form of faith. [60] For example, there is the temptation to overcome feelings of inferiority and guilt by identifying oneself with what Jung call the persona. This mask is not the true person but is that of oneself which one shows to others. The person with inferiority and guilt feelings may create the persona of the righteous man and then unconsciously see it as his true person. This is not hypocrisy in the usual sense of the term, for it is an unconscious camouflage of the true self, even from one's own self. Hutton also mentions these neurotic, quasi-religious reactions as the partial explanation of religious fanaticism. [61] The various forms of spurious faith afford little protection against the emotional dejection arising from aloneness, but the communion that comes through genuine faith prevents a man from feeling absolutely alone.

The awareness that one is loved by God and daily, personal communion with God are powerful antidotes for loneliness. Yet man needs human society. God said of Adam, "It is not good that the man should be alone." Even in religious communion not only *koinonia* with God is necessary but also *koinonia* with other believers by which each supports and builds up the faith of the other. The unmarried, too, need those communions which most people find in marriage. The church by providing fellowship upon a religious basis can supply these needs in part, for in the church there is opportunity for a communion of sexes, generations, individuals, milieus, and personalities. [62] Intimate personal friendships are also very rewarding for many older unmarried people. Many of the benefits and communions of marriage can be had in such a relationship. Friendship, however, since it does not involve any legal tie, contract, financial dependence or social demand of the one upon the other, is much more vulnerable to destructive influences than marriage. Seldom is it as lasting or as productive of a sense of security as marriage. Yet, says Harding, there are friendships "sufficiently important to warrant the formation of a family or household unit ... [and] the values of such a relationship, the daily companionship, the shared life interest, the 'home' are in many ways comparable to those found in marriage." [63]

Such friendship, especially if it develops into love of an emotional character, can be very beneficial, but it is socially suspect. Mead says that unmarried men who even share the same apartment "have to fend

---

[60]   *De Ongehuwde Vrouw,* pp. 106, 107.

[61]   *Ibid.*

[62]   The social obligation of the church toward the older unmarried will be discussed in chapter four.

[63]   *Op. cit.* pp. 108–111.

off very heavy doubts as to their heterosexuality" and "as for the households in which two unmarried women live together, they are still regarded with a tolerance that includes some of the last century's pity and absolution from blame of the woman who did not marry, but this is markedly decreasing." [64] Society today identifies emotional love and sexuality. [65] But emotional love does not necessarily mean that there is a sexual involvement or even sexual desires or reactions. [66] Love and sex are not the same thing, nor does one necessarily include the other. For unmarried persons who have no sexual expression, the suppressed instinct may color their relationship and lead them to conscious sexual impulses and even overtly sexual acts, but such is not a necessary outcome.

Since the older unmarried are being excluded from the American family, friendship with persons of the same sex and of the other sex is one of the most valuable means for overcoming the isolation of the older unmarried and thus for mitigating the effects and problems of singleness. Society generally and the church in particular must be hesitant in making an adverse judgment upon such friendships and the living arrangement evolving out of them. New customs and social forms are necessary when society makes a significant change like the redefinition of the family. Brunner's admonition is applicable here also: "morality does not always break down at the point proclaimed by the puritanical, and only too often the Church has made the mistake of simply siding with the defenders of the old order against the growth of newer and perhaps better customs." [67]

The Sexual Problem of the Older Unmarried

"So God created man in his own image, in the image of God created he him; male and female created he them." Every person from creation on is either a male sexual being or a female sexual being. The human person is inescapably sexual. Among other things this sexual nature of man means that each person has a sex drive whose demands intend to be met. The sex drive is a powerful motivation and as such plays an

---

[64] *Male and Female*, pp. 326, 327.

[65] Derrick S. Bailey cites a good example of this identification. The relationship of David and Jonathan described in I Samuel 20 is commonly interpreted as a homosexual one although there are no exegetical grounds for such an interpretation. The Old Testament represents them as normal, heterosexual men. Both married, David, polygamously, and had children. No "special significance [should] ... be attached to the oriental vehemence with which both men expressed their emotions when they parted company ... ," *Homosexuality and the Western Christian Tradition*, London, Longmans and Green, 1955, p. 56.

[66] Theodor Reik, who after thirty years parted with Freud on the libido theory, thoroughly analyzes Freud's identification of love, the emotions, and sex in *A Psychologist Looks at Love*, New York, Farrar and Rinehart, 1944. Cf. especially pp. 7–25.

[67] *Op. cit.*, p. 378.

important role in the life of every normal human being, young or old, married or unmarried. It is the propulsion which brings two people together out of their aloneness and joins them together in such a way that they are not merely two individuals in relation but are welded together into a unity, the two become one. [68] And through this sex drive comes a further blessing, children. [69]

Inherent in singleness is the problem of what is to be done with this divinely created, deeply rooted, powerfully motivating sex drive. This is a physical, biological problem, but it is more. This is a psychic problem, a social problem, a moral problem, but it is still more. It is a religious problem: it is part of the problem of man's true relation to God, of his religious response of faith to God's call, of his role in the kingdom in this world but not of this world. In dealing with this problem the church in her ministry to the older unmarried is confronted especially with the danger of moralism: the reduction of the problem to a question of right and wrong, the approach to an unmarried person only as judge. This is the legalism of the Scribes and the Pharisees which Christ condemned. The sexual problems of the older unmarried should not be considered in isolation from justification through faith, sanctification through faith, God's love and forgiveness, and the gift of the Holy Spirit who imparts both enlightenment and power to the believer. The church's ministry does not exclude the moral judgment, the question of rightness and wrongness, but is diametrically opposed to any reduction of the problem simply to this aspect. Necessary above all is the love described by Paul in I Corinthians 13 and exemplified by Jesus in his conversation with the Samaritan woman and with the woman taken in adultery. [70] Morality in and of itself is not a spiritual good any more than is economic wealth. It must be morality in Christ, for the kingdom's sake, as Christ pointed out to the rich young ruler who had obeyed the commandments from his youth on. He had yet to deny himself in order to follow Jesus. [71] Both the older unmarried and the church must remember not to place the final emphasis upon moral purity in their treatment of these sexual problems but upon salvation

---

[68]   The sex act in itself brings about a unity. Paul says that even a man who has sexual intercourse with a prostitute becomes one body with her, I Cor. 6 : 16. This is not the only unity or the highest unity that can exist between man and woman, but nevertheless it is a real unity of two people achieved through sexual intercourse. See Otto Piper, *The Christian Interpretation of Sex*, pp. 40–47.

[69]   Biblically seen, the conception of children is not simply the purpose of sexual intercourse nor simply the result of it, but a blessing, a gift, added to the sex act. Cf. Psalm 127 : 3 and 128 : 3, 4. The Bible does not deny a causal connection between sexual intercourse and conception but neither does it make conception the purpose of coitus. Therefore, in setting forth the Biblical evaluation of sexuality and the sex drive, the concept of procreation will be decidedly of secondary import.

[70]   John 4 : 7–26 and 8 : 1–11.

[71]   Mark 10 : 21.

through faith, that Christ forgives the sins of those who believe in him and gives to them eternal life. This eternal life which has been given them is the kingdom with its blessings, which they can and must serve in whatever situation or state they find themselves: married or unmarried, slave or free, Jew or gentile, [72] and with all the powers and abilities that God has given them, their sex drive included. To begin anywhere else than with justification through faith and the gift of eternal life and to attempt to solve this very real and pressing problem apart from the forgiveness of sins and the incorporation into Christ is an implicit denial of the Biblical emphasis of the Reformation and a reversion to a concept of a sanctification which comes in some way and to some degree other than from Christ through faith. [73] True self-denial, also that of the sex drive, is a fruit of the gift of eternal life and has as its purpose service in the kingdom.

This kingdom-oriented self-denial is the theme also of Jesus' words to the disciples recorded in Matthew 19 : 10—12. When the disciples concluded that a man had better not marry if he could not divorce his wife except for adultery, Jesus lifted the question of singleness versus marriage off the level of *to sumpheron,* an individualistic ethic of personal happiness, to that of *dia ten basileian ton ouranon,* for the sake of the kingdom of heaven. The sexual self-denial of the older unmarried must be kingdom-motivated, whether they are voluntarily or involuntarily single. The significance of this passage must not be limited to those who have voluntarily relinquished marriage in order to perform some special kingdom service. When Jesus said, "Not all men can receive this precept, but only those to whom it is given," the *ois detotai* refers simply to those who are citizens of this heavenly kingdom, as Jesus states in Matthew 13 : 11. [74] The distinction is not "some in the kingdom who are able to receive this precept" and "others in the kingdom who are not able" but "those who are in the kingdom" and "those who are not in the kingdom." Only those who are in the kingdom are able to receive this precept, that a man can remain unmarried for the sake of the kingdom of heaven. The point of this pericope is not the specialness of the *charisma* of which Paul speaks in I Corinthians 7 : 7, but that only through citizenship in the kingdom with both its blessings and its obligations of service should the normal man remain unmarried. The point is not the ability or inability to

---

[72] I Cor. 7 : 17—24. See chapter two for the discussion of this passage.

[73] See R. Schippers, *De Gereformeerde Zede,* Kampen, J. H. Kok, 1955, for an excellent discussion of the Christian calling to the ascetic life in which he carefully avoids both antinomianism and legalism by accenting both justification and the gifts of eternal life. See also G. C. Berkouwer, *Faith and Sanctification,* Grand Rapids, Eerdmans, 1952, pp. 17—44, in which he discusses the relation of faith and justification to sanctification and pp. 109, 110, where he handles Lord's Day 44 of the Heidelberg Catechism.

[74] Cf. F. W. Grosheide, *Het Heilig Evangelie Volgens Mattheus,* second edition, Kampen, J. H. Kok, 1954, p. 291.

remain unmarried because of a person's sex drive, but the individualistic versus the kingdom motivation. The interpretation of the last part of verse 12, "He who is able to receive this, let him receive it," in terms of the having or not having of the *charisma* mentioned in I Corinthians 7 : 7 tends to shift the emphasis from that which is the point of this pericope. These three verses state simply the possibility of kingdom-motivated singleness and Jesus' approval of it and by implication his disapproval of an individualistically motivated singleness.

The *charismata,* also that of continence, are blessings of the kingdom, within which it is possible to remain single with the right motivation. These ,charismata come from God purely through his grace, as the word *charisma* itself states. They are specific, individual gifts: "All these are inspired by one and the same Spirit, who apportions to each one individually as he wills." [75] They are not given for the happiness, ease, or satisfaction of the person himself, but for the common good, [76] for the establishment of the kingdom by service of others. [77] Schippers sums up these elements in his definition of *charisma* as "a special gift of the Holy Spirit in the new dispensation intended to serve the extension of the kingdom of God." [78] This description is true also of the *charisma* of continence. It, too, is a specific, individual, unmerited spiritual gift received from the Holy Spirit with a kingdom purpose.

Care must be taken to avoid a one-sided interpretation of these *charismata.* Although they are spiritual gifts, they have a natural, developmental aspect, for the supernatural does not exclude the natural, nor the ictic the processional. For example, when Paul calls his deliverance from mortal danger a *charisma,* [79] he does not deny that created powers, personal or impersonal, may have been involved in a, scientifically speaking, causative way in this deliverance. The same is true of other *charismata.* As MacDonald points out, the modern man would likely interpret many of the *charismata* named in the New Testament as natural gifts and capacities only heightened or quickened by the power of Christ, but for the early Christians "not only was the basis of their salvation objective; the process of its completion" including all the gifts, powers, and services through which this was accomplished was also seen as completely a work of God. [80] That the *charisma* of continence is a gift, and a spiritual one, does not exclude the role of temperament, personality, character, and even glandular balances in the

---

[75]   I Cor. 12 : 11. See also I Cor. 7 : 7 and Rom. 12 : 6.

[76]   I Cor. 12 : 7.

[77]   I Cor. 14 : 26.

[78]   "... een bijzondere gave van de Heilige Geest in de nieuwe bedeling be-stemd om de uitbreiding van het rijk Gods te dienen," *Gereformeerde Zede,* pp. 229, 230. (Translation mine, M. H.)

[79]   II Cor. 1 : 11.

[80]   *Christian Worship in the Primitive Church,* Edinburgh, T. and T. Clark, 1934, pp. 44, 45. All three of these, *charismata, diakonia,* and *energemata,* are spoken of as "manifestations of the Spirit for the common good," I Cor. 12 : 4–7.

achievement of continence. Neither can it be reduced to these factors. It is spiritual, but it must not be spiritualized. It is a gift, but it does not come mechanically, nor does it operate mechanically. Its being a gift of grace does not exclude the processional involvement of man and nature. This processional involvement means that the gift must be exercised, trained, used, and developed. [81] Such an understanding of *charisma* does not reduce the role of God in matters such as prophecy, faith, or continence but extends it, for that which modern man calls natural is God's activity too.

The preceding description of *charisma*, though far from complete, provides the necessary background for the interpretation of Paul's reference to the *charisma* of continence in I Corinthians 7 : 7. Significantly, only in this verse, only in this general statement about all spiritual gifts does Paul use the concept *charisma*. When he speaks of the decision to remain single or to marry, the deciding factor is the exercise of self-control, *egkrateuesthai*. [82] Paul is undoubtedly thinking of the *donum continentiae*. [83] This sexual self-control is a gift of grace which some have received and others have not. [84] Yet his naming it the exercise of self-control rules out any mechanical concept of this gift.

In this chapter Paul is evidently answering the question of the Corinthian church, should we marry or remain single? The question of the involuntarily single and the problem of their control of the sex drive is not directly considered in this chapter. Yet it may reasonably be asked if Paul's statement that no one should decide to remain unmarried unless he is able to exercise self-control and his statement that this self-control is a *charisma* do not have implications also for the sexual problems of the involuntarily single. Does not Paul implicitly say that the possibility of sexual self-control for the single person, voluntarily or involuntarily single, depends not upon himself but upon the grace of God, that is, upon a *charisma?* From Paul's statement that they who do not have this gift of self-control should marry, it should not be concluded, however, that the involuntarily single have an unsolvable problem. This would be tantamount to saying that in some situations or states a person has no other choice but to sin. This would be directly contrary to what Paul says in verses 17–24. The involuntarily single can never say, "I do not have the gift of self-control and I cannot marry, so I am compelled to sin."

This chapter should not be interpreted in isolation from what Paul

---

[81] See Rom. 12 : 6, *"Having gifts* that differ according to the grace given to us, *let us use them";* I Peter 4 : 10, "As each *has received* a gift, *employ it* for one another, as good stewards of God's varied grace"; and I Tim. 4 : 14, "Do not neglect the gift you have."

[82] V. 9.

[83] Cf. F. W. Grosheide, *Eerste Brief aan de Kerk te Korinthe*, second edition, Kampen, J. H. Kok, 1957, p. 186.

[84] V. 7.

writes a few chapters later, "No temptation has overtaken you that is not common to man. God is faithful, and he will not let you be tempted beyond your strength, but with the temptation will also provide the way of escape, that you may be able to endure it." [85] Also relevant are such passages as "the Lord knows how to rescue the Godly from trial" [86] and "For because he himself [Jesus] has suffered and been tempted, he is able to help those who are tempted." [87] The unmarried can and must pray for this gift of self-control in the faith that God will also provide the way of escape, that they may be able to endure the temptation. But this prayer must not be self-centered. The gift of self-control has, as have all *charismata,* a religious and not simply a moral purpose. It is given for the extension of the kingdom, the overcoming of sin in this world through the salvation of Christ. Nor is its primary purpose self-edification but the common good, [88] since through this gift they can give their undivided interest to the Lord. [89]

Concretely, the Scriptural passages exegeted above mean that the older unmarried man and woman must see that they have two and only two choices as answers to their sexual desire: either marry or live the life of self-control. They cannot shed their responsibility for their sexual activities because self-control is an unearned gift any more than an unbeliever is relieved of his responsibility because faith is a gift. Those single persons for whom the first alternative—marriage—is no longer a real possibility must still make a conscious decision to follow the second way of life, the way of self-denial, and to follow it for the sake of the kingdom. This is no irrevocable decision should the opportunity for marriage arise later, but it is a necessary decision for the development of self-control until that time comes.

Nor can the unmarried escape their responsibility by an appeal to a "right of sex experience." Sex experience is not a good which can be divorced from the responsibility which goes with it. The sex act is a good only as it serves the divine purpose of joining two people together in a marriage unity. Only within this union is there a right of sex experience. There is in American society, including the psychiatrists and counselors who write on the problems of the unmarried, a widespread opinion that sex experience is a human right because it is natural to human nature. They feel it is natural to have sexual intercourse and unnatural to live without it. Many who hold this view would hesitate to give an unqualified approval of extramarital sex experience, but they still regard celibacy as a state inconsistent with human nature. One form which this opinion commonly takes today is the argument that

---

85   I Cor. 10 : 13.
86   II Peter 2 : 9.
87   Heb. 2 : 18.
88   I Cor. 12 : 7.
89   I Cor. 7 : 32—34.

sexual experience is an inescapable need. [90] Either the very possibility of celibacy is doubted, or it is argued that celibacy has dire physical and psychic ill effects. As yet, neither of these alternatives has been proved. Both of them, as van den Berg points out, [91] are often based upon the assumption that a healthy man or woman has a certain fixed quantity of drive to expend. If he does not expend this drive in some form of sexual activity, then he does it in cultural activities through sublimation, and if not in these then in various kinds of neuroses. However, it has not been proved that there is a fixed quantity of chemical stuff given off by the organs of the body which produces a corresponding, thus just as fixed, quantity of sexual drive, which the individual must in some way discharge. [92] The validity of such a position is doubtful. [93] Yet from it arises the commonly held conviction that celibacy is detrimental to psychic and possibly also physical health. Although not enough research has been done in medicine, psychiatry, and other allied fields to determine the symptoms and effects of celibacy in the older unmarried, [94] many accept this modern position uncritically. If adequate proof were given to support the proposition that celibacy often or even always has physical or psychic ill effects, such as more than normal nervous tensions, irritability, and concentration disturbances, which can be traced simply and directly to the biological frustration of the sex drive, sexual experience would not thereby be justified for the unmarried person. There are demands and obligations which are higher than psychic or physical health, higher even than life itself. The fulfillment of many duties and obligations, including marriage and family obligations, causes psychic and physical strain which can adversely affect health, but these obligations overrule the duty to care for one's health.

Nor does it follow that man has an inescapable, intrinsic need for the satisfaction of his sexual desires because complete celibacy is an unknown phenomenon in this world. Even if it could be shown that there is no known case of complete celibacy among normal men and women, this proof would in no way substantiate a "right of sex experience." Man is not simply an instinctual creature but a responsible being,

---

[90] This common opinion is found in many scientific works. E.g., Kinsey operates on this assumption in both his books on sexual behavior. See Alfred C. Kinsey et al., *Sexual Behavior in the Human Male*, Philadelphia, W. B. Saunders, 1948, pp. 206, 207.

[91] "Man en Vrouw," *Wending*, July/August, 1954, p. 277.

[92] *Ibid.*

[93] Many psychologists attack these assumptions as biological reductionism. Cf. Karen Horney, *op. cit.*, ch. 3, "The Libido Theory," especially pp. 55, 56, and Kardiner, *Sex and Morality*, p. 121.

[94] Most studies to date, such as K. B. Davis, *Factors in the Sex Life of 2200 Women*, New York, Harper's, 1929, and. R. L. Dickinson and L. Beam, *The Single Woman*, Baltimore, Williams and Wilkins, 1934, are concerned with the range of normality rather than singleness and celibacy *per se*.

created able and obliged to rule his instincts. That it is not possible for him always to do so is a result of sin, but this impossibility does not invalidate his responsibility and give him a right to satisfy his desire. An example will clarify this. Perfect and complete honesty is an impossibility in this world. Psychologically, lying can be explained as a means of self-protection. The need for psychic security drives every man at some time to conceal the truth from others because he feels that their knowledge of it would threaten his existence. The loss of the respect of others would lead to a loss of self-respect. These facts, however, do not give a man the right to an intentional misrepresentation of the truth. The unattainability of perfection is no validation of imperfection.

The choice of the way of self-control is the acceptance of the full responsibility for one's life. This choice must be a conscious, well-considered, freely accepted decision. No other person can accept their responsibility for them, they must accept it themselves. This kind of choice is necessary not only for the voluntarily single but also for the involutarily single, for whom the first alternative, marriage, is not a real possibility. This choice is not an acceptance in the sense of "being resigned to my fate" or "being satisfied with my lot" but an active embracing of one's obligations in his particular situation or state. It is not the fate, the lot, the unsatisfied desire, that is accepted, but the obligation to serve God in this state. Therefore, there is no irrevocable decision to live a life of sexual self-denial, should the opportunity for marriage later arise. The decision is not to be celibate *per se*, but in the state of singleness to serve God through celibacy, to be celibate that the kingdom might come. Both the voluntarily single and the involuntarily single person must become the voluntary, kingdom-purposed eunuch of whom Jesus spoke in Matthew 19. This is the message of the church to the older unmarried in answer to his sex problem.

In practice, this way of self-control means that the older unmarried must not seek to live out their sexual desires, to express them and to find a certain satisfaction of them in the male-female interaction of looks, glances, thoughts, suggestions, connotative gestures, etc., which have their place for those who belong to the group of yet-to-marry. The unmarried must give such a form to his life that his sexual desires are not being stimulated in the way that they are and should be for a married person. The married person, too, must give a certain form to his life so that sexual demands adequate for marriage are realized. Psychotherapeutic practice repeatedly proves that this latter form is

---

[95] M. B. Smith makes the unsupported statement "Continence and health are evidently not workable for *all* human beings or for the large majority," *The Single Woman of Today*, London, Watts, 1951, p. 48. Brunner says, also without substantiation, that "only in rare cases can it [the sex drive] remain unsatisfied without causing disturbances of a physical, psychic, and spiritual nature," *op. cit.*, p. 366.

also not easy for all people. [96] For those who have chosen the way of marriage there is a laudable and pure sexual interest in the members of the other sex, but for the single who have decided to follow the way of the *donum continentiae*, this very interest must be denied. Living the life of self-control demands training in the sense in which Paul spoke of training himself in order to have a clear conscience before God and before men. [97] Since this *donum continentiae* does not work mechanically, the unmarried must exercise their self-control, also by avoiding the intentional stimulation of the drive.

The older unmarried do not lose their sexual drive through the exercise of self-control—or, otherwise stated, through this *donum continentiae*. Whether the force of the drive is even diminished is a question still being debated. The gift of God is the control, not the annihilation of the drive. Neither the older unmarried nor their fellow Christians who are ministering to them should in any way underrate the power of this drive or be overly optimistic about the ease of its control. The gift of self-control is not given to a man full-blown. It must develop and grow. Even after choosing the way of self-control the single person may find himself overwhelmed by sexual urges. The *charisma* of continence is no more an absolute guarantee of chastity than the gift of Truth is of continual and complete honesty. Contemplation of the radical sinfulness of the human heart should destroy any false hopes of perfectionism and prevent any puritanistic amazement and shock at failure. That stubbornness of sin of which Paul spoke in Romans 7 : 15—20 is evident also in the sexual life of man. [98]

Social and psychic factors reinforce that sinful proclivity in the sexual life of the older unmarried. The sexual instinct is especially amenable to cultural influences because it is not an instinct in the same sense that hunger and thirst are. Even though it has a biological basis, its satisfaction can be delayed, distorted, or entirely abrogated. Its force can also be motivated and stimulated in a multitude of ways. [99]

For the older unmarried two of the most common influences upon the strength of the sex drive and the ability to control it [100] are social

---

[96]   van den Berg, *op. cit.*, p. 278.

[97]   Acts 24 : 16.

[98]   It is perhaps especially evident in the sexual life of man. Notice how consistently, prominently, and extensively the sexual sins of the unbelievers and of the church are mentioned. See, e.g., Rom. 1 : 24—32; I Cor. 5 : 1, 6 : 9; Gal. 5 : 19, 20; and I Tim. 8 : 9, 10. This emphasis may have been occasioned by the historical situation of the early church, but it may also show something of the tremendous power of sin in the sexual life of man.

[99]   Therefore it is often classed as a secondary instinct, as does G. H. Seward, *Sex and the Social Order*, Middlesex. Penguin Books, 1954, p. 2, to distinguish it from the truly unlearned and goal-directed behavior. A. Kardiner, *op. cit.*, p. 99, points out that only because the sexual instinct is not an instinct in the elementary sense can we speak of a person's psychosexual development.

[100]   These are mentioned together because they are relative to each other.

isolation and society's high evaluation of sexual satisfaction. The older unmarried in their exercise of self-control must take into account these two inhibiting factors. The church, too, in her ministry to them must seek to overcome both these elements.

The person who is socially isolated has a much greater difficulty controlling his sexual urges. Not only do these desires command a greater part of his attention and interest than they would if he had strong social relations and interests, but sexual contact also becomes a means of making social contact, a way to overcome aloneness. Karen Horney explains the influence of isolation in this way. Isolation instills anxiety. Just as a child becomes afraid when he is left alone, so the mature man needs social contact and companionship to feel secure. It is not the demand for satisfaction so much as the "necessity for obtaining reassurance against a lurking anxiety which lends ... strivings their strength and tenacity. People can renounce food, money, attention, affection so long as they are only renouncing satisfaction, but they cannot renounce these things if without them they would be or feel in danger of destitution or starvation or of being helplessly exposed to hostility, in other words, if they would lose their feeling of safety." Since isolation is an inducement to this feeling of insecurity, it is a powerful inhibition to the control of sexual desires. [101] The influence of isolation can also be described in terms of compensatory motivation. In most people social isolation raises self-doubts. They question their value and usefulness since no one seems to need or desire their company. Since sexual acts—whether the solitary acts of fantasy and masturbation or the sexual acts in which another person is involved—can be used to compensate for lacks in other areas of life, [102] these doubts become strong motivations to compensatory sexual activity.

Society's high evaluation of sexual satisfaction, described in chapter two, also has a strong negative influence upon the single person's attempt at self-control. When a healthy sex life is equated with regular and as-complete-as-possible satisfaction of the sex drive and when the healthy sex life, so defined, is seen as a basic condition to the achievement of a well-developed personality and a happy, well-adjusted, productive life, the social pressure upon the older unmarried person to satisfy his sex drive is strong. Renunciation and self-denial are no longer social ideals, as they were in the Middle Ages. The instincts must be expressed,

---

There is no way of measuring the absolute strength of the sex drive. One can only speak of its strength in relation to its control.

[101] *New Ways in Psychoanalysis*, pp. 73–75. See also Wijngaarden, *Gesprekken met Uzelf*, pp. 177, 178.

[102] Kardiner discusses these compensatory motivations of sexual acts in *Sex and Morality*, pp. 32, 33. The Don Juan who flits from one sexual conquest to another is an example of a person for whom the dominant motivation for the sex act is non-sexual. He is seeking not sexual satisfaction as an end in itself but support for his self-esteem. These conquests are repeated self-assurances that he is not a failure.

gratified, and even satiated. Of course, modern society does not allow complete free play of instincts and drives. As every other society, it demands that these drives be met within certain social forms and only under certain circumstances. But modern society says these desires must be met, especially the sexual desire because of its central importance in the life of man.

Theodor Reik, however, correctly adds that much of what appears to be a high social evaluation of sexual satisfaction is actually a high evaluation of romantic love. [103] When society says "how can you blame anyone who is deeply and desperately in love," "love justifies all," and "man's highest responsibility is to answer to the love imperative," it is romantic love of which it speaks. However, this romantic love is no longer identified with platonic love. The sex act is seen as a very important part of the romantic relationship between a man and a woman. Therefore, the satisfaction of the sex drive gains a good part of its social value from the halo around romantic love. The net effect is still a social pressure upon the older unmarried which undermines their efforts for chastity. It strengthens the force of temptation by adding a strong, social, non-sexual motivation to an already powerful sex drive.

To the older unmarried, troubled and tempted by their sexual desires, the church of Christ must bring a message not just of obligation but also of forgiveness, not just of law but also of grace. The mercy and goodness and faithfulness of God must be proclaimed to them. In short, the full gospel must be brought. The realization that they are justified through faith alone and not in any way by their moral purity must permeate their lives. The training of self for the life of self-control must rest upon the conviction that they are reconciled with God. Both the church in her ministry and the older unmarried in their exertions to live the Christian life must carefully avoid any separation of sanctification from justification, for such a separation is disastrous also for their training of self. The pure life comes through faith and love, through a restored relationship to God—that is, through justification. Although the gospel contains warnings and admonitions, the proclamation of forgiveness is the power to the new life.

Thurneysen rightly calls the church to the proclamation of the unconditionality of forgiveness in her ministry to the sinner. She must not fear to proclaim the generosity and inexhaustibility of God's grace. She must dare to bring an uncleansed sinner into the presence of God, because this forgiveness is the source of the pure life, or the life in Christ. [104] This is what Jesus meant when he said that only the man in the kingdom will be able to receive this saying, the saying that a man

---

[103] *Of Love and Lust*, New York, Farrar, Strauss, and Cudahy, 1957, pp. 369–373.

[104] *Die Lehre von der Seelsorge*, pp. 143, 144 and 146, 147.

can make himself a eunuch for the sake of the kingdom of heaven. This is part of what Paul meant when he called continence a *charisma,* for a *charisma* is a blessing of salvation. Self-control comes through forgiveness.

The realization of guilt arising from the sexual practices of the unmarried man or woman has a disturbing effect upon that person's religious response to God, upon his entire spiritual life. His consciously realized guilt stands as a barrier between him and his God and restrains prayer, praise, worship, and communion. David described his spiritual aridity under the burden of guilt in Psalm 32 : 3, 4: "When I kept silence, my bones waxed old through my roaring all the day long. For day and night thy hand was heavy upon me: my moisture is turned into the drought of summer." Sin is a disturbance in man's relationship to his God. This disturbance undermines faith and raises his susceptibility to temptation, for the sinner cuts himself off from the sanctifying power of God. True confession, since it includes faith, and also faith in God's infinite mercy, integrally contains the awareness of forgiveness. The awareness comes with the forgiveness just as justification comes with and through the conscious awareness of it in faith. This true confession is sometimes extremely difficult for the person who in spite of his resolutions to break with a particular sin repeatedly succumbs to the same temptations. Some unmarried persons become despondent or, even worse, indifferent when sin follows forgiveness seemingly as inevitably as forgiveness follows sin. To them must be brought the message of God's free, unearned, and unlimited mercy to the sinner. Their faith must be strengthened through the reassurance that God forgives not seven times but seventy times seven. Through this proclamation in the church's ministry their response of faith and service is restored.

On the other hand, there is one very real sense in which it is wrong both psychologically and spiritually to say, "I lay my sins on Jesus" or "Satan caused me to sin." Either can be a projection of guilt and responsibility, through which the person seeks to justify himself and in this way allay his guilt feelings. He must be brought to the realization that though he was tempted by Satan, *he* is responsible for *his own* sin and though Christ assumes the guilt, it is *his* guilt that Christ removes. Neither demonic influence nor divine forgiveness negates personal responsibility.

Nor is the proclamation of forgiveness just a psychotherapeutic means of strengthening the will by overcoming anxiety. The certainty and knowledge of forgiveness does not provide the power to resist temptation whether forgiveness has actually occured or not. It is the forgiveness itself, as an act of God, that accomplishes the new life. But this forgiveness does not operate apart from the awareness of its occurence, that is, apart from faith. It is not the faith, but the object of faith that gives the power to resist and change. But since the power comes through faith, the heart of the church's ministry to the older unmarried who are faced with sexual problems is, as is always her ministry, the proclamation of the gospel.

Heterosexual Intercourse

Many specific problems of the older unmarried need closer examination. These particular problems are attempted answers for the general sexual problem of "what shall I do with my sexual desires?" The person who has extensive personal contact with the older unmarried will frequently meet these problems. Recent surveys such as those of Kinsey have shown that the sexual activity of single people is much more extensive than was commonly thought. The basic solution to these problems has already been sketched in the preceding section. Although the several elements of the Christian answer to this problem of life will not be repeated, they form the foundation of the ministry to the unmarried involved also in these various sexual activities. Yet these sexual problems must be individually considered in their social and psychic aspects. A consistently Biblical ministry recognizes that man and his society are organically involved in the process of salvation and that social and psychic factors influence a man's total response to the gospel. In her ministry the church will, therefore, seek to determine these factors and will work to change those which adversely affect the Christian life and, until changed, to minimize their effect.

One answer to the sexual problem inherent in singleness is heterosexual relations outside of marriage. If Kinsey's statistics can be taken as indicative of the sexual experience of American men and women, [105] most single men and women not only have the inclination and opportunity but at some time in their life have heterosexual intercourse. The accumulative incidence—that is, the percentage who have ever had heterosexual intercourse—for single men at the age of 35 was found to

---

[105] Kinsey admits, pp. 22, 23, *Sexual Behavior in the Human Female*, Philadelphia, W. B. Saunders, 1953, that his sampling is not strictly representative of the whole population. It was not possible to get a sample of each age, social, economic, and educational group proportional to the American population. In some cases he has omitted the data of groups of interviews which were found to be unrepresentative of the American population, as for example the sexual histories of prison inmates. For some tables he attempts an adjustment according to the total population breakdown. The accuracy of his data can be questioned also because of the relatively small number of interviews, less than 20,000 out of a total population of over 160,000,000. The chief bias of his data results from his method of selection of subjects. This was inevitable because he could only interview those who were willing to co-operate. But the possibility is great that those who were uninhibited enough to give details about their sex life are not representative of the population as a whole. Even though absolutely correct sampling might modify Kinsey's final percentages, his work is the most extensive and possibly the most accurate available today.

be 87 percent [106] and for single women at the same age 48 percent. [107] For many of these heterosexual intercourse is no single, isolated experience. About 40 percent of the single women over 40 years were having heterosexual intercourse regularly with a median frequency of slightly over once per month. [108] These figures include, however, many who were engaged and were having sexual intercourse with fiancees. The picture of the sex life of the single woman as she is defined in this thesis would probably be modified. However, the active incidence for the ages 46–50 is still 34 percent [109] and this very likely includes few engaged persons. Although strong religious convictions lower both the accumulative incidence and the active incidence, 30 percent of the devout Protestant single women over 35 have had heterosexual intercourse—still much lower than the 63 percent incidence of inactive Protestants. In every respect the figures are higher for men. For example, the active incidence of heterosexual intercourse of single men 40 years old was found to be about 70 percent and the mean frequency was over once per week. [110] A study of 4,600 unmarried draftees by Hohman and Schaffner generally confirms these statistics. They found that 79.4 percent of the single men they questioned had had heterosexual relations. [111]

If these statistics are generally correct, about four out of five older unmarried men and one out of two older unmarried women at some time in their lives have had sexual relations with the other sex and about three out of five single men and three out of ten single women are continuing such relations, although some sporadically. These high percentages reveal heterosexual intercourse to be one of the most common sexual problems of the older unmarried.

The Christian who recognizes Scripture as the norm of life as well as of faith cannot concede what Harding describes as the general public opinion, that "women who are self-supporting are at liberty to run their own lives as they please, provided that they injure no one and preserve an outward aspect of respectability . . . [That is, if] they behave decorously in public, do not obtrude their love affairs in an objectionable fashion, safeguard themselves adequately both from scandal and from pregnancy, the rest is their own affair; the exact degree of intimacy between themselves and their men friends is no one's business." [112] The believer cannot accept this *laissez faire* attitude because by his commitment to Christ he is concerned about the spiritual welfare of his fellow-

---

[106] Alfred C. Kinsey et al., *Sexual Behavior of the Human Male*, Philadelphia, W. B. Saunders, 1948, p. 550.

[107] *Human Female*, p. 333.

[108] *Ibid.*, p. 288.

[109] *Ibid.*

[110] *Human Male*, p. 708.

[111] Leslie B. Hohman and Bertram Schaffner, "The Sex Live of Unmarried Men," *American Journal of Sociology*, May, 1957, pp. 503 and 505.

[112] *The Way of All Women*, p. 259.

man, believer or unbeliever, also when this spiritual welfare is involved in problems touching the most intimate, private, and personal areas of life.

Such concern demands an understanding of the import of heterosexual relations for the older unmarried person. These questions must be asked and answered. Why are so many single men and women drawn into heterosexual affairs? Why is the percentage so large even for those who are convinced that it is wrong? What psychic and social needs or desires does it satisfy? Are these legitimate desires? If so, are there other ways to satisfaction harmonious with the believing response to the gospel, or must these desires be suppressed in spite of their legitimacy?

Heterosexual intercourse does not necessarily have a sexual motivation. If there is a sexual motivation, it is not necessarily the dominant one. The psychologist Abram Kardiner says that just because it is possible to love without having sexual desires and to have sexual desires without loving, sex can also be a vehicle for emotions and attitudes other than love. The sexual act can be an expression of the desire to dominate, the desire to submit, the need of self-respect, and feelings of pride. [113] And any activity in which pride is involved can become the vehicle for compensatory activity. The man who has a low opinion of himself because he considers himself a failure in business, in society, or even in his religion may seek his self-esteem by sexual conquests. These conquests become a way of establishing status. Social factors also play a role. Society presses the single man to prove his virility. His singleness casts doubts upon his virility unless he can convince others that though single he is sexually active. Boasting may quiet society's doubts, but it does not quiet his own. He joins the rest of society in including virility as an essential characteristic of masculinity. He feels that coitus is the only way in which he can prove to himself that he is a complete man. If a woman feels inferior to others for whatever reason, neurotic or realistic, the achievement of an affair with a man whom she admires can give a strong compensatory satisfaction. Since the older unmarried woman often has extensive inferiority feelings as a result of society's adverse evaluation of her, she is especially tempted to use sexual intercourse as a compensation. The sex act can also be a means of self-degradation as the result of guilt feelings. In this way she humbles and punishes herself. [114] Or sexual intercourse can be a means of self-reassurance of her sexual potency and desirability. [115] Since the single woman, with the rest of society, tends to doubt her sexual desirability and capacity because she is still single, the sexual act is seen as an opportune means of self-reassurance. [116] Reik cites the case of an

---

[113]   *Sex and Morality*, p. 32.

[114]   *Ibid.*, p. 33.

[115]   *Ibid.*

[116]   See also A. H. Maslow, "Self-esteem (Dominance Feeling) and Sexuality in Women," *Journal of Social Psychology*, Vol. 16, 1942, pp. 259–294. He, too, concludes that in the emotionally insecure the motivation for extra-marital affairs is not primarily sexual but is a search for security through self-reassurance.

unmarried woman who had a series of sexual affairs in which the primary motivation was the need to convince herself that she was attractive and could be loved by men. [117] Deutsch in her book *The Psychology of Woman* [118] agrees that sexual acts do not necessarily arise from "genuine sexual need." Therefore it is possible for a sexually frigid woman to desire and carry out an affair with deep satisfaction. Dickinson and Beam cite several cases of women who entered into sexual affairs from a dominant motive other than sexual. One woman forty-six years old experimented "perhaps as much from curiosity about life as sexual desire." [119] For another woman the sexual affair was motivated by her maternal desire. She chose younger men so that she could mother them. She always hoped that these affairs would lead to marriage, but again the motivation was primarily maternal. Marriage was only a means of having children. [120] These cases illustrate Kardiner's conclusions that sexual intercourse "can be used to implement any dominant motivation of the personality." [121]

The psychic, non-sexual significance of heterosexual intercourse is even greater for the affair than for the isolated, perfunctory, individual sexual experience. The affair has a history, a development—a present, a past, and possibly a future. It is more deliberate, for it gives the opportunity for reflection and for allowing the conscience to play a role in the actual experience, not just as an accuser after it is over. The meaning of the affair can be contemplated and its desired goal can be defined. Reflections upon personal motives and those of the lover are possible and usual. In contrast to the solitary sexual experience the affair must be justified, at least in part, in the mind of the person involved while it is being carried on, or there must be motivations strong enough to overcome the objections of society and conscience. The non-sexual motivations are more persistent and constant than the sexual one and therefore better sustain the development and continuation of the affair. Also, in the affair there is more opportunity for emotional involvement and thus satisfaction of these non-sexual desires. Hutton correctly concludes that in spite of the conflicts and anxiety which arise in the affair because it is not a contract confirmed by society and possibly not approved by their own conscience, it can give deep psychic satisfaction because it is a well-developed, nuanced emotional relationship. [122] As a result, when the affair is in the process of breaking up—as it usually does, for one reason or another, about two or three years after it began [123]—and when the emotional attachment has weakened or

---

117   *Of Love and Lust,* pp. 387, 388.
118   Vol. 1, p. 40.
119   *The Single Woman,* p. 173.
120   *Ibid.,* pp. 189, 190.
121   *Op. cit.,* p. 33.
122   *De Ongehuwde Vrouw,* p. 65.
123   Dickinson and Beam, *The Single Woman,* p. 166.

disappeared, leaving only the sexual attachment, most of the meaning and satisfaction of the affair has also disappeared. Particularly the woman feels this way about a fading affair because she finds it more difficult to divorce her sexual desire from her emotional reactions.

Since the stronger motivations are generally non-sexual, it is not easy for the older unmarried to break up an affair in spite of ambivalent feelings toward the relationship, the feeling of insecurity, fear for reputation, fear of pregnancy, and guilt feelings. The reinforcing motivations are non-sexual, and since the condemnation of conscience and society is centered on the sexual aspect of the relationship, these motivations are but little affected. If the affair is broken off, the single man or woman finds it difficult to resist being involved in a subsequent affair. Over half of the group studied by Dickinson and Beam had subsequent affairs, although usually not for a year or several years later. [124] The time lapse is to be explained in part by the emotional adjustment after the first affair ended, which was necessary because the affair was not merely a sexual relationship but also an emotional one.

For the unmarried, one of the most important non-sexual motivations for the affair and, to a lesser extent, for the single sexual contact is the need to overcome their aloneness. As Piper points out, [125] one of the divine purposes of sexual differentiation and of the sex drive is to overcome the danger which lies in the mere fact of human individuality. Man was created a person, able to make concious decisions and determine his own life, but he was not created for his own self but for others. Woman was taken out of him—that is, sexual differentiation and sexual attraction was created in the creation of woman—to overcome the aloneness with its temptation to self-sufficiency and self-complacency. This purpose of sexuality was imbedded in the nature of the sexual relationship. The breaking down of isolation is one of the functions of the sex drive. The older unmarried man and woman today are not alone in the absolute sense that Adam, the only man on earth, was alone and yet their aloneness has in it something of that of Adam. In the single sexual contact and especially in the sexual affair they see the possibility of overcoming their aloneness, their feeling of dissatisfaction with self, their loneliness, and their sense of purposelessness. The aloneness which qualifies the entire life of the older unmarried qualifies also their sexual life. Only within human relationships can they find satisfaction for their legitimate desires: their desire for a child, their desire to belong to someone, their need of security, their need of self-assurance, etc. And they seek it in that human relationship in which most persons find satisfaction of these desires and which society says is basic for the happy life and the development of their

---

[124] Op. cit., pp. 172–174.
[125] The Christian Interpretation of Sex, pp. 95, 96.

personalities: the intimate male-female relationship of which sexual activity is a part.

Since the sex drive is no more the only motivation for the affair than it is for marriage, any attempt to help the older unmarried man or woman which limits its concern to the sexual desire will quite likely fail. Attention must also be paid to the other desires which are being satisfied. These other motivations for the sex act are not always self-evident. One of the methods of psychotherapy can be very valuable for the discovery of the subjective meaning of these sexual contacts. If the single person finds it difficult or impossible to articulate the various desires being satisfied in sexual intercourse, he should be encouraged to talk freely and uninhibitedly not only about these various experiences but also about other emotional experiences, needs, and desires. His sexual experiences are not isolated sections of his life but a part of the whole. The motivations driving him to sexual intercourse will also come to expression in other experiences and aspects of his life. For example, the woman for whom the sexual affair is predominantly a means for the satisfaction of her maternal desire will also reveal this motivation and its vast importance for her in many subtile and overt ways. She may have chosen a profession which gives her extensive contact with children. She may constantly seek opportunities to fondle, care for, and play with children. She may, by speaking disparagingly of the parental abilities of her married sisters or friends, reveal her jealousy of women who already have families. The single person may be totally unaware that these desires are significant personal motives for his sexual activity. The desire itself may be unconscious or only semi-conscious. Or, if conscious, its role as a motivation for sexual contact may be unconscious. The pastoral conversation must make use of this method of psychotherapy in the ministry to the older unmarried caught in these problems. [126]

Masturbation

Masturbation is another of the common attempted answers to the sexual problem of the older unmarried. Kinsey found that the active incidence for the single male between the ages of 36 and 40 was 57.7 percent [127] and for the single female of the same age group 54 percent. [128] Although these two percentages are nearly the same for both the single man and the single woman, there is a significant difference in the behavior patterns. For single women the active incidence reaches its peak at the age of forty and decreases only slightly from then until old age. For single men, however, the active incidence, according to

---

[126] The pastoral conversation and its use of uninhibited verbal expression will be discussed in chapter 4.

[127] *Human Male*, p. 240. See also p. 471.

[128] *Human Female*, pp. 144, 145.

Kinsey, reaches a peak of 88 percent in the mid-teens and drops steadily from then into old age. [129]

Masturbation may have a very simple, biological motivation. It may be only the physical means of obtaining physical satisfaction of a biological drive. Usually, however, the deeper, concomitant motivation is of another character. Since the sex drive is readily joined to other wishes, inclinations, and strivings, various other psychic drives may impel the person to the act of masturbation. Many psychologists and psychiatrists name inferiority feelings as the most common non-sexual motivation of masturbation. [130] It is a form of substitutive compensation to which a person resorts when things go wrong. It is used as a method of self-comfort and of preservation of self-esteem. Chessar cites an example of a man who used masturbation in this way when his emotional life was disturbed. Masturbation was a substitution for a threatening reality. [131] The motivation of inferiority feelings is often evident in the fantasies which commonly accompany masturbation. According to Kinsey, 64 percent of the females who masturbated at least sometimes had accompanying fantasies and 50 percent almost always had accompanying fantasies. [132] These fantasies are usually overtly sexual, but not necessarily so. They may also be imagined events or pictures in which his or her own person is being punished (masochistic tendency), is punishing someone else (sadistic tendency), or is shown to be superior or successful and consequently is greatly admired (inferiority feelings). In all of these the dominant motivation revealed in the fantasy is non-sexual, even though the fantasy event may be sexual. For example, the person who doubts his or her attractiveness to the other sex and has resultant inferiority feelings, may act out a compensating fantasy of sexual intercourse, even rape, with some real person whose admiration he greatly desires or with an ideal person who exists only in his imagination. The satisfaction that he acquires from this fantasy and the accompanying act of masturbation is in a large measure the allaying of inferiority feelings. A very serious result of such fantasies, whether they accompany masturbation or not, says Weatherhead, [133] is that on occasion these persons assert the actual occurrence of events that took place only in fantasy. Such neurotic delusions are not uncommon, but if unrecognized as delusions, they can have disastrous social

---

[129]   *Ibid.* These figures must not be taken as the percentage of single men or women who are at any one time engaged in the practice of masturbation, for the active incidence was computed for a five year period and had it been calculated for a one year period, the active incidences in most instances would have been lower, says Kinsey, *ibid.*, p. 47.

[130]   Cf. A. Kuypers, *Inleiding in de Zielkunde*, Kampen, J. H. Kok, 1953, pp. 286, 287, and Eustace Chessar, *Sexual Behavior: Normal and Abnormal*, London, Medical Publications, 1949, p. 124.

[131]   *Op. cit.*, pp. 128, 129.

[132]   *Human Female*, p. 189.

[133]   *The Mastery of Sex*, p. 107.

consequences for the person they accuse. The person engaged in the pastoral conversation with the person with neurotic tendencies is often the object of his or her delusions because of the emotional tie resulting from transference. [134]

The older unmarried, especially single women, often doubt their attractiveness to the other sex. This is a common fear in modern society where millions are spent to alleviate these doubts, but the single woman has more reason to doubt because of society's verdict of her. These doubts of self-value, coupled with a high estimation of the value of sexual satisfaction and fears of the ill effects of celibacy, provide a strong non-sexual motivation to masturbation. Her social isolation intensifies her inferiority feelings and her self-doubts. Any attempts to break this habit and any counsel given to one caught in the habit of masturbation must take serious account of these psychic motivations, for as long as these psychic needs are not gratified or at least consciously acknowledged, this act and its accompanying fantasies will be such an important source of the person's feeling of well-being that the habit can hardly be broken, except by a very strong contrary motivation.

Two other psychic phenomena intensify this problem: guilt feelings and fear of psychic and physical ill effects. An interesting discovery has been made by psychotherapists, pastors, teachers, and others who have dealt with the sexual problems of single persons: as long as a person feels guilty about the practice or fears harmful consequences, he or she will engage in it more frequently. When the fear or guilt is removed, the activity is moderated or stopped. [135] Shield's statement of the effect of fear may be taken as typical of the opinion of psychotherapists: "... it is no exaggeration to say that the habit has been riveted on many boys ... by the indiscreet and scientifically inaccurate threatenings of the terrible things that would happen if it were persisted in." [136] Several explanations of this effect have been advanced. Kardiner attributes it to a defeatist attitude: the person feels that if he is going to be punished, he may as well have all the fun he can get. [137] This cannot be the full explanation, for many struggle against the temptation but still repeat the act almost as by compulsion. Waterink explains it as the inhibiting effect of guilt and fear upon the will. [138] Whatever the psychological explanation, both fear and guilt feelings result in increased masturbatory activity. To those caught in this vicious cycle it must be carefully but emphatically explained that masturbation itself seldom or never has psychic or physical ill effects.

---

[134]   The phenomenon of transference will be discussed in chapter 4.
[135]   Cf., e.g., Kardiner, op. cit., p. 127.
[136]   "The Adolescent Boy," Sex in Social Life, S. Neville-Rolfe (ed.), p. 265.
[137]   Op. cit., p. 127.
[138]   Puberteit, Wageningen, Gebr. Zomer en Keuning, [1955], fifth edition, pp. 143—145,

Physically, it has an effect similar to that of an equivalent amount of sexual intercourse and no more. [139] Psychically, masturbation does not lead to emotional disturbances, but the fear and anxiety engendered by the belief that it has such an effect may do so. The effect of misinformation, superstition, and threatening advice must be negated by frank personal discussion.

The fixation of the habit caused by guilt feelings can sometimes be traced to exaggerated or neurotic guilt feelings. If they are a neurotic symptom, treatment by a trained psychotherapist is necessary. Other persistent guilt feelings spring from a lack of trust in God's unlimited and unmerited mercy, through which come both forgiveness and the power to resist sin. God is as ready to forgive the repeated sin as the solitary sin. His forgiveness does not require purity; it is the source of purity. The new life is realized through forgiveness and the ministry of the church is the gospel of this forgiveness, through which comes the clearance of guilt.

As long as the attempt to overcome temptation is thought of as primarily a great moral battle for purity, the ability to resist is undermined. When the attention is limited to the struggle to overcome the habit and its sinfulness, the more fixed becomes the habit. Any morbid introspection, whether in prayer or contemplation, only increases the tenacity, for it turns the attention to the activity and this attention produces guilt feelings and new temptation. [140] The guilt must never be seen apart from God's mercy, through which comes the purification of life.

But neither must these guilt feelings be quieted by justifying the practice. Acceptance of the practice as an unimportant, normal, necessary biological act may have the psychic effect of making the need to masturbate less urgent and thus will bring some relief from the compulsion. But the act of masturbation is not simply a biological process. The whole person is involved. It is a responsible action in which his desires, attitudes, and motives are expressed. An individualistic ethic which excludes censure because it is a solitary act which harms no one, fails to recognize that masturbation uses for solitary pleasure that which was created for a social use, for the forming of that community between two people called marriage. On the other hand, there is no ground for judging the act more severely than other forms of self-indulgence. Waterink pointedly remarks that effective therapy includes the understanding and conviction that one's guilt for this sin differs in no way from that of other sins which are concerned with the satisfaction of physical stimuli, such as eating too much, or drinking too much. [141] The more serious sin lies in the fantasies which accompany

---

[139] Shield, op. cit., p. 266, and Hutton, "The Unmarried," Sex in Social Life, Neville-Rolfe (ed.), p. 57.
[140] Cf. Weatherhead, Mastery of Sex, pp. 107 ff.
[141] Puberteit, pp. 144–145.

the act. Here the words of Jesus about him who looks after a woman to lust after her are applicable.

Homosexual Intercourse

The inclusion of this subject in a study of the older unmarried is not meant to imply either that a significant percentage of the unmarried are sexually abnormal (a modern social judgment handled in chapter two) nor that all homosexual persons are unmarried. This subject is included because homosexual intercourse is one of the attempted answers of the older unmarried to their sexual problem. Since the immediate goal of sexual activity is orgastic pleasure, not procreation, the object to which the sex drive is directed can be changed. The male sexual partner can be exchanged for female and the female for male. Such homosexual practices occur especially when there is sustained contact with members of the same sex and some segregation from eligible members of the other sex. This situation is found, for example, in the army and in boarding schools, and the higher incidence of homosexual practices in both of these is well-known. The older unmarried person often comes into close intimate contact with other unmarried persons of the same sex. Not infrequently do they share living quarters in private homes, apartments, boarding houses, or YMCA's or YWCA's. An intimate emotional friendship either prior or subsequent to the decision to share an apartment, a home, or rented rooms is also not uncommon, especially for unmarried women. This friendship can be very beneficial to them psychically, socially, and religiously for through it they overcome part of their aloneness. However, their sexuality may play a role in their relationship, especially when there is no other avenue of expression and when their sexual desires have not been consciously recognized and acknowledged, but are instead repressed. This can occur even though neither of the two may be conscious of the mutual sexual stimulation and satisfaction. [142] Even though this aspect of their relationship may remain unconscious and unexpressed in specifically sexual acts, even for long periods of time, it can easily lead to conscious homosexual desires and homosexual practices.

These are normal, heterosexual people involved in homosexual activities. Their disposition or psychic structure is such that under other circumstances their sex drive would be directed to the other sex. Subjectively, the homosexual act may be for them a heterosexual deed. Although the act objectively is homosexual, in their imaginative fantasy accompanying the deed they are having coitus with some real or ideal person of the other sex. It is questionable whether one can accurately call these people homosexual, for although their deeds are homosexual, their psychic structure and possibly also their desires and intentions

---

[142] Hutton, *De Ongehuwde Vrouw*, p. 71.

are heterosexual. The invert, or genuine homosexual, is a person who from either hereditary or acquired and either biological or psychic causes [143] has a psychic structure which directs his sex drive to members of the same sex. The sexual attraction he feels is predominantly or completely for the same sex. A clear distinction between these two types is very necessary for the church's ministry, for her approach to the two will be considerably different. The person ministering to these people must realize that not all who engage in homosexual practices are genuine homosexual persons nor do all genuinely homosexual persons commit homosexual acts. Homosexuality "is not, as commonly supposed, a kind of *conduct;* it simply denotes in male or female a *condition* characterized by an emotional and physico-sexual propensity towards others of the same sex." [144]

The ministry to the heterosexual older unmarried person who engages in homosexual practices and/or has homosexual desires does not differ essentially from the ministry to the older unmarried person who engages in heterosexual fantasies and/or heterosexual intercourse. Both the single homosexual act and the homosexual affair can have as many and as varied non-sexual psychic motivations as the heterosexual act or affair. The maternal instinct, the desire for love and companionship, and inferiority feelings may be the dominant motivation or a strong supporting motivation. The subjective significance of these acts and affairs must be determined in the same way as that of the heterosexual act or affair. Again, the fear that the relationship will be broken up by the other party since there is no social or legal bond to hold it together over difficult periods gives the affair a franticness, rigidity, and possessiveness which makes the relationship assume unnatural importance, so that they can hardly extract themselves even if they feel guilty about the relationship.

The church in her ministry must recognize one social factor that is peculiar to this sexual problem. The average heterosexual person has

---

[143] The influence of heredity and biological processes is not yet determined. Hamer says that there is as yet little positive support for the theory of innate homosexuality or for a causal relation between brain and nerve conditions or deviations of glandular secretions and homosexuality. *Zielzorg en Psychiatrie,* p. 151.

[144] Bailey, *Homosexuality and the Western Christian Tradition,* p. x. The church's ministry to the genuinely homosexual person is a very interesting and important problem, but it is not strictly a part of this thesis. By no means all inverts remain unmarried since the sex drive is certainly not the only, nor necessarily the dominant, motivation for marriage. There are pseudo-heterosexual persons as well as pseudo-homosexual. B. J. Stokvis cites the cases of at least three homosexual persons who married. Cf. *De Homosexueelen,* Lochem, "De Tijdstroom," 1939, pp. 139 and 154. Also, although the condition of homosexuality is often a cause of singleness which affects other areas of life, including the religious, it cannot be considered in this thesis. Treatment of it and other causes of the same category, such as physical deformities and neuroses, would lead us too far afield. An excellent book laying down the Biblical basis for the church's ministry to the genuinely homosexual person is that of Bailey, cited above.

a strong negative emotional reaction to homosexual practices and, through the identification of conduct and condition, to homosexuality. The homosexual act is regarded as particularly loathsome and repulsive. There is a curious disparity between the judgment of homosexual practices and heterosexual sins such as adultery, prostitution, and fornication. Bailey suggests that the irrational, emotional repulsion to the condition, homosexuality, stems from a horrer of the homosexual act, since these are usually identified, and that the repulsion to this act can be traced to the traditional Western view of woman and marriage. The language historically used to describe the homosexual act is revealing: "playing the woman" and "using a man like a woman." It suggests that the act is a degradation more of the male because he is acting like a woman than of human nature as such. Fornication or adultery, on the other hand, at least prove a man's virility. This underlying reason also explains why male homosexuality is so severely condemned and female homosexuality has received so little attention that it has scarcely ever been mentioned by church councils or secular law. [145] Reik concurs in this analysis of the emotional reaction to homosexuality and especially male homosexuality. "Women as well as men judge female homosexuality in a milder way than the male perversion." The reason for this disparity is that male "homosexuals have, in our often unconscious opinion, renounced the privileges of their masculinity and virility." [146] The deed is judged from a high valuation of masculinity as compared with femininity, not from a moral or religious point of view.

Such an irrational, emotional reaction inhibits the church's ministry to both the heterosexual person involved in homosexual practices and to the genuine homosexual, who may or may not engage in homosexual deeds. Any expression of this emotional reaction, even though it be non-verbal and unconscious, will block the confidences necessary for personal ministry to the individual. If the person does confide his or her problem to another, this emotional reaction blocks the unrestricted proclamation of God's love and mercy to the sinner. Finally, the social attitude to the person engaging in homosexual acts, whether he or she is homosexual or heterosexual, isolates this person from personal communion, except for communion with others involved in the same practices. Both the isolation itself and the forced communion with others involved in homosexual practices provide added cause for the continuation of such activities. Not only are they isolated by society when their acts and/or condition is known or suspected, they isolate themselves out of fear of discovery. [147] This emotionally enforced

---

[145]   Bailey, op. cit., pp. 161–164.

[146]   Of Love and Lust, p. 507.

[147]   Cf. Stokvis, De Homosexueelen, p. 56. This book, containing 35 short autobiographies, was used as a primary source for the various motivations of homosexual conduct and the effect of social attitudes.

isolation from society can have a devastating effect upon the person's religious response to God. It makes the homosexual affair assume extraordinary proportions, for this is all they have in life. This is their only society, their only love, their only purpose. It becomes a fixation from which they cannot free themselves. Were they accepted by society, by the church, and by their families in Christian love, mercy, and true concern for their welfare, this inclination to transgress God's law would lose one of its strongest impulsions. The Christian must overcome his irrational, emotional repulsion to the homosexual act and to the condition, homosexuality, so that these people may be drawn back into society and especially the society of the church.

Both the prevention and treatment of pseudo-homosexuality requires the conscious acceptance of the sex drive and sexual desires. Neither the direction nor the expression of the drive or desire can be controlled as long as it is unconsciously repressed. The older unmarried must recognize and acknowledge their sexual desire and consciously decide to deny its satisfaction if the alternative of marriage is voluntarily or involuntarily excluded.

Involuntary Sexual Mental Images and Desires

The older unmarried have one spiritual problem related to their sex life which arises regardless of the extent of their self-control. Apart from any conscious activity of the will and sometimes even against what the person consciously wills, mental images and thoughts with a sexual content will enter the consciousness and sexual desires will arise. No matter how forcefully they struggle to suppress these mental images and desires, they recur again and again. The statement of Jesus in the sermon on the mount "But I say to you that everyone who looks at a woman lustfully has already committed adultery with her in his heart" [148] seems to condemn them, no matter how valiant their efforts. Although the problem of the mental images, the thoughts, and the desires lies in their apparent involuntariness, they are not to be explained as the same psychic phenomenon nor to be judged alike, even though they are all sexual. No sexual thoughts, mental images, and desires are sinful *just because they are sexual,* any more for the unmarried than for the married person. The sex instinct is native to man and he will react sexually to certain stimuli in certain situations. This sexual response, both mental and sensual, is the product of one of the basic drives, those most elementary powers that underlie longings, inclinations, wishes, and desires. The drives are not in themselves perceivable, but are expressed in the above mentioned forms. [149] Neither the drive

---

[148]   Matt. 5 : 28.
[149]   Cf. the article "Drift" by R. Schippers and J. de Jong in *Encyclopedie van het Christendom,* Protestants Deel, pp. 317, 318, upon which this discussion of basic drives was based.

nor expression of the drive in these forms is sinful. "Sex desire is not wrong and Jesus did not say so. To cast any aspersion on sex desire is to impugn the integrity of the Creator and of his creation." [150]

The question that then arises for the older unmarried person who has chosen the way of self-denial is this: if the drive is good, if sexual response is inevitable for the normal person, and if these mental images, thoughts, and desires arise in spite of my conscious will, am I morally and religiously responsible for them? The answer to this question must be carefully Biblical: it must avoid both moralism and a denial of the depravity of the whole man. Weatherhead settles this problem by asserting that these thoughts and desires are never sinful until the person willfully retains them in the consciousness and gives conscious assent to them. [151] Such a position is contrary to the Biblical emphasis of the Reformation upon the tenth commandment, "Thou shalt not covet . . . ," which forbids any desire contrary to the other command- ments of God. Yet it is necessary to distinguish between desire and lascivious desire. Murray sums up the Biblical teaching on this problem: "sex desire is not wrong" nor is it "wrong to desire to satisfy sex desire and impulse. . . . What is wrong is the earliest and most rudimentary desire to satisfy the impulse to the sex act outside the estate of matrimony. It is not wrong to desire the sex act with the person who may be contemplated as spouse if and when the estate of matrimony will have been entered upon with him or her." [152] However, Wijn- gaarden's further clarification must also be remembered: the sexual receptivity of a person is not limited to the actual or prospective marriage partner. One's sexuality can be awakened by others than the love partner. This sexual response is neither wrong nor sinful but the expression of a healthy and complete life. [153]

Løgstrup makes a further contribution by distinguishing between sexual drive and the individual, personal form (*selbstischen Gestalt*) which each man gives to this drive. [154] The drive itself is not evil nor is sexual desire outside of marriage in itself sinful, but the *Gestalt* which the person gives to this drive when it is expressed in longings, desires, and wishes may be sinful. Not the giving of *Gestalt* is sinful, for this is unavoidable, but a *Gestalt* contrary to God's commandments. This is what Jesus condemned in Matthew 5 : 28. This man had given a sinful *Gestalt* to his sexual drive by directing it to a woman when either he or the woman was already joined to another in marriage. Jesus does not condemn looking at the person of the other sex nor, as Schippers says in *Gereformeerde Zede*, [155] the erotic response stimulated by the

150   John Murray, *Principles of Conduct*, London, Tyndale Press, 1957, p. 56.
151   *Mastery of Sex*, p. 107.
152   *Loc. cit.*
153   *Hoofdproblemen*, p. 223.
154   "Eros und Ethos," *Zeitschrift für Evangelische Ethik*, January, 1958, p. 6.
155   Pp. 120, 121.

person of the other sex. Rather, our looking and our desire must be cleansed by the love of Christ. It must be given new *Gestalt:* new direction and new purpose.

The older unmarried should also distinguish between sexual and erotic attraction and desire. Not all attraction between the sexes is sexual. A man may feel strongly attracted to a married woman, for example, and greatly desire her company without his sexual desire being active. This is erotic attraction. Waterink defines it as an admiration and diffidence for a member of the other sex which has nothing to do with sexuality. The admiration is of a spiritual nature. It is one of the esthetic feelings, a love of the good, the true, and the beautiful. [156] The single person must take care not to devaluate erotic attraction by misjudging it as lacivious desire. He may and should admire the good and beautiful personal qualities of those he meets, whether these characteristics are physical, psychic, or spiritual. Waterink gives a clarifying example of erotic attraction. In the early years of puberty boys often engage in hero worship. Their feeling of insufficiency leads them to seek someone who embodies all those qualities which they greatly admire. The resulting emotional bond is not at all sexual; it is purely erotic—though a sexual attraction may be added to it. [157] The single person must, however, be on his guard that the erotic attraction does not lead to a sexual involvement and sin on this level, for the emotional bond created through erotic attraction provides an eminently suitable climate for the development of a sexual affair. [158]

Mental images and thoughts with a sexual content which arise apart from or even contrary to the conscious activity of the will must yet be considered. These two are not to be judged alike because they are not the same psychic act. Sexual mental images arising involuntarily are to be explained by the psychic phenomenon called association. Certain situations, objects, ideas, words, etc. have a sexual association because through some experience in the past a connecting bond has been formed between the two mental images. When the non-sexual mental image later occurs in the mind, the sexual image comes into the consciousness by an automatic psychic reflex action. These associations are simply involuntarily recalled memories, even though the original experience that forged the bond has been forgotten. As mental images rising from the memory, they are no more to be judged than any other mental image acquired from reading a book, hearing a news broadcast, or seeing some event. The older unmarried person must not be disturbed by the presence of these sexual images arising in his consciousness by association for they are a normal and necessary phenomenon. Without it, learning and even thought itself is impossible. However, mental images are not the same as thoughts. In thinking, the

---

[156] *Puberteit,* pp. 134, 135.
[157] *Ibid.*
[158] *Ibid.*

person, the "I" in the narrow sense of the responsible religious center of men, is involved. The "I" forms thoughts, just as it gives *Gestalt* to desires. This distinction is readily evident in an example: the word "adultery" produces a mental image of a sinful sexual act. This mental image is neither moral nor religious. It is even necessary for the understanding of the seventh commandment. The person's attitude or response to this mental image in his thoughts is moral, not neutral or natural. This mental process may be sinful.

For these desires and thoughts which have a form, a direction, and a purpose contrary to the demands of God, the unmarried person must seek forgiveness and through the forgiveness, cleansing. But he must not regard the mere presence of sexual desire or sexual mental images as sinful. The danger of prudery is real for the person who is training himself in the way of self-denial. But prudery has nothing in common with Christianity. Gallichan gives a penetrating insight when he says that prudery and pornography are related in their attitude to sex. It is sacred to neither but rather inherently vulgar, obscene, and impure. The only difference is that the one reacts positively, the other negatively.[159]

This attitude to sexual desires and sexual thoughts may lead the older unmarried person to an attempt to repress these thoughts and desires. He may deny the existence of his sexual drive and its various manifestations. This is far from an ideal state for the older unmarried. Harding calls this "ostrich psychology" and warns that "a deliberate assumption of unconsciousness leaves one vulnerable at every weakest spot." [160] When a person refuses conscious recognition of this powerful force because he feels guilty about it, he shuts out the possibility of true control. Suppression, or self-denial, on the other hand, does not annihilate sexual thoughts or desires, nor does it exclude them from the consciousness but rather frankly recognizes their exact nature and then denies these desires satisfaction outside of marriage.

---

159   *The Poison of Prudery*, New Castle-upon-Tyne, n. p., 1929, p. 31.
160   *The Way of All Women*, pp. 126, 127.

CHAPTER IV

THE SPECIFIC FORMS OF THE CHURCH'S MINISTRY TO THE OLDER UNMARRIED

Introduction

The preceding chapters were concerned with those problems of the older unmarried which hinder the realization of a life of reconciliation to God through faith in Jesus Christ, directed according to the revealed will of God and devoted to his service. The problems were analyzed, their effect upon a life of faith and service was noted, and various solutions were proposed. These chapters emphasized the personal responsibility of the older unmarried to recognize their problems and personally accept a solution productive of the life of faith and service. The role of the church in effecting these solutions and the methods open to her must yet be considered.

The basic content of the church's ministry to the older unmarried is the same as that of her ministry to any other group. It is the ministry of the gospel of salvation and eternal life through Jesus Christ. The form which the ministry takes is determined in a large part by the social and psychic conditions of the group to which it is directed. Some of these conditions and their influence upon the spiritual life of this group have been described in the preceding chapters.

There is great need for more sociological and psychological studies of the older unmarried. Only the broad outlines of the social attitudes to the unmarried, of social expectations of this group, and of their actual function in American society could be sketched in this thesis. Very little work has been done in either sociology or psychology on the unmarried man. In psychology more work must be done on the emotional effects of celibacy and on neurosis as a cause of singleness. The effect of these neurotic causes upon the later life of the single person also needs study. [1] When the results of these studies are presented, the theologian must determine the effects of these conditions upon the spiritual response of the older unmarried and seek the form of the church's ministry which will help them achieve the full Christian life.

In this final chapter some conclusions for the church's ministry to this

---

[1] Edmund Bergler, a noted American psychiatrist, has made a preliminary study of neuroses in the unmarried. He concludes that aversion to marriage is very often a sypmtom of neurosis. Reported by John E. Gibson, "How Neurotic Are You?" *Ladies' Home Journal*, March, 1958, pp. 47, 48.

group will be drawn on the basis of the social and psychic factors described in the preceding chapters. Not only the general character of her ministry will be stated, but some concrete solutions will be weighed.

The Church's Proclamation of Social Judgment

Embedded in American society are various concepts which harm the older unmarried. These concepts determine social attitudes and thus shape the patterns of social intercourse. The church may not uncritically conform to social patterns, attitudes, and premises. She may never forget that she is unique, that she has a vertical dimension which determines her nature, her faith, and her life. Therefore, she must place under the judgment of the Word the culture in which she lives and of which she is a part. She must never fear to go against the tendencies of public life. In her ministry to the older unmarried she must counteract those elements in American society which inhibit and warp the single person's response to the gospel of *shalom.*

The church must proclaim God's judgment of social attitudes. The ridicule, discrimination, derision, and—at best—indifference with which society regards the single woman must receive the church's uncompromising condemnation. She must lay bare the pride that lies at the heart of these attitudes.

The church must proclaim God's judgment of social patterns. Society closes the door on the unmarried women; and, though some force their way back into society by accomplishments too brilliant to be ignored, the weaker stand outside public life, looking in. Yet, society is beginning to make room for new patterns of sexual activity. The public tends to overlook sexual affairs of single men and, to a lesser degree, single women. But the church may not simply take over these social patterns. She must protest against them and seek to change them.

And the church must proclaim God's judgment of society's premises about marriage, sex, and the single woman. Here the church comes to the heart of the problem of the unmarried woman. The single woman is regarded a failure; she is seen as incomplete and inferior because she did not marry. Society proceeds on the assumption that woman has an absolute obligation to marry and raise a family. Against this assumption stand the words of Paul and of Jesus that earthly relationships, including the marriage relationship, are of secondary importance. They are not finally determinative of man's duty or value. In the new dispensation the believer-believer relationship overshadows the man-wife and the parent-child relationships. The church must place earthly relationships in their proper perspective by making known man's ultimate purpose and by giving a sober, calm evaluation of marriage and its role in realizing this purpose. She must judge modern man's fanatic concern for human relations—a concern isolated from the balancing concern for his divine relationship. The church must also instill in society a different concept of marriage and sex. Sexual satisfaction is not the most important benefit of marriage. It is not basic to harmony and happiness in all the other aspects of the marriage relationship. Society's sense of the exaggerated importance of sexual activity and satisfaction for marriage and for life generally, must be overcome. For the judgment of society's premises the church needs Paul's eschatological orientation; from a kingdom consciousness she gains the necessary perspective to make correct evaluations.

The church must proclaim her judgments of social attitudes, social patterns, and social premises in the congregation. This proclamation must be included in her preaching, in her catechetical instruction, and in her ministry to the individual. She must begin with her own body; but she may not stop there. She has to witness also to those of society who are not part of her body. To change the attitudes, patterns, evaluations, and premises of society she must witness to the whole society whenever and wherever she can find opportunity. In the press, in literature, on radio and television, on the stage, and in the public pronouncements of her governing bodies she must work to accomplish these changes by proclaiming the secondary importance of earthly relationships, the provisionality of this life, and the eschewal of total involvement in the relationships of this earth.

This task cannot be left to the preacher, the elder, and the deacon; to the consistory, the classis, and the synod. Every member of the church must become a prophet. He must protest against every misrepresentation of the true value and purpose of man—male and female, of marriage, and of sex. And he must become active in those mediums which form public opinion.

Through the proclamation of the whole church to the whole society social attitudes, patterns, judgments, and premises can be changed, and the situation of the older unmarried can be bettered.

The Church's Task Within Existing Social Patterns

The church functions within the general pattern of society. Even when she is making a serious attempt to change elements of this pattern, she has to take into account the pattern then existing and has to work within it. Given the present social attitudes, patterns, and premises, how can she best minister to the needs of the older unmarried?

The most obvious and possibly the most comprehensive answer to the problems of this group has not yet been considered. It is marriage. Some psychotherapists and theologians regard marriage as either the primary or the only solution to the problems of singleness. J. W. Herfst, a woman pastor who is herself unmarried, says the problem of the older unmarried is in principle unsolvable, unless its solution be found in marriage itself. [2]

---

[2] "De Ongehuwde Vrouw," *Wending*, July/August, 1954, p. 384.

Gallichan does not even consider other solutions. He restricts his proposals to ways of encouraging a higher marriage rate: the abolition of poverty, the change of social attitudes toward love and marriage, and a relaxation of divorce laws to encourage the hesitant. [3] Emil Brunner strongly emphasizes marriages as the answer to the problems of the unmarried, even though he recognizes both the secondary importance of marital status and the extraordinary opportunities of the single for service. Therefore he calls Christians to overcome those social and political forces which limit marriage. [4]

Marriage is a legitimate and commendable solution. Paul not only refuses to call marriage a sin, [5] but he honors marriage as a holy state [6] and denounces those who forbid it. [7] In the same context in which he upholds singleness as an honorable state providing the possibility of extraordinary service, he advises marriage as a legitimate and even commendatory answer to the problems of many people. [8] The unmarried have, at least theoretically, two possibilities: the service of God in marriage or the service in singleness through the exercise of self-control.

But since this first possibility is only theoretical for many unmarried, the question arises: should the church be concerned to make this a real possibility? Does the church have a pastoral obligation to provide these with the possibility of marriage in so far as she is able? Is their finding a mate and their marrying a problem proper to the church with her peculiar nature and purpose? Paul thought so. He advised Timothy to encourage the younger widows to marry and raise a family. [9] And Paul states the reason for his apostolic concern—that is, the reason why he, an apostle of the Christian church, writes Timothy, a minister of the gospel, to include in his ministry to the younger widows a recommendation to marry. Paul says that for the younger widows widowhood is a state which gives occasion for sin and which, in turn, hinders the witness of the church: "they learn to be idlers, gadding about from house to house, and not only idlers but gossips and busybodies, saying what they should not," and in this way they give the enemy occasion to revile us. [10] Although marriage is by no means essential for salvation and for service in the kingdom, for some people singleness and all that it involves is an obstacle to the full Christian life. This inhibiting influence is not a necessary effect of singleness, but is a possible one; therefore the recommendation of marriage is a legitimate part of the ministry of the church to the individual.

---

[3] *The Great Unmarried*, London, T. Werner Laurie, [1916], pp. 140—175.
[4] *The Divine Imperative*, pp. 364—366.
[5] I Cor. 7 : 28. See also vs. 2, 9, and 38.
[6] Eph. 5 : 21—33.
[7] I Tim. 4 : 1—3.
[8] I Cor. 7.
[9] I Tim. 5 : 14.
[10] I Tim. 5 : 13, 14.

The decision to remain single or to marry is completely that of the single person himself. He must decide in which state he can better serve God. His decision is not based on whether or not he can remain sinless in the unmarried state—for example, whether he can achieve complete control of his sexual desires—for complete purity is not a possibility in marriage either. His question is: does God ask of me service in singleness or service in marriage? The church does not make the decision for him. Her ministry consists of the promotion of self-conscious, responsible decision.

But does her ministry end here? If a person has responsibly decided that he or she must marry, does the church have a further obligation when the possibility of marriage is only theoretical? Should she go beyond the promotion of responsible decision and, in specific circumstances, the recommendation of marriage, to the point of helping them find a mate and thus realize their decision?

The Hervormde Kerk (the Dutch Reformed Church) considered this problem, and in 1951 its Raad voor Kerk en Gezin (Council for Church and Family) instituted a marriage contact bureau. [11] This bureau has as its stated purpose the promotion of contact between older men and women who want to marry but have not found a mate because their occupation, place of residence, or other conditions have limited marital opportunities. [12] The further goal of the bureau is, of course, the promotion of marriage, and its ultimate goal is the promotion of the Christian life. E. L. Smelik, one of the moving forces behind the institution of this bureau, stated the motive impelling the Council in an article introducing the bureau to pastors and laymen. [13] He said, although some single persons, because of their psychic structure, are content to remain unmarried, others feel a strong need for marriage. Singleness per se is neither a fate nor cross, but it is such for some individuals. The wish of those who deeply desire marriage may not be refused on the ground that the single person is also a volwaardig mens. Therefore, an obligation exists to help them marry.

But why must the church do this service? Both Smelik [14] and Ruitenberg [15] give as primary reasons the insufficiency and unreliability of existing means. There remains in society a great, unfilled need in spite of the many ordinary and extraordinary means of answering it. Secondly, many of the existing means are untrustworthy. Marital advertisements

---

[11] Cf. *Hervormd Huwelijks-contactbureau,* a brochure published by the bureau. It is available by writing Postbus 5032, Scheveningen.

[12] *Ibid.,* p. 2. Cf. also E. L. Smelik, "Een Belangrijk Pastoraal Initiatief," *Weekblad der Nederlandse Hervormde Kerk,* Oct. 13, 1951, pp. 153, 154 and Oct. 20, 1951, pp. 157, 158.

[13] *Op. cit.,* Oct. 13, p. 153. Cf. also L. H. Ruitenberg, "Huwelijksbemiddeling," *Wending,* Oct., 1954, pp. 509–513.

[14] *Ibid.*

[15] *Op. cit.,* pp. 509, 510.

in newspapers or magazines [16] often lead to deception, swindles, and heterosexual or homosexual affairs. Marriage bureaus already exist, but the personnel of some have insufficient psychological and sociological training and the method of others is superficial and irresponsible. Either they fail to collect the necessary information about their clients, or they are not sufficiently confidential in their operation, or in a determined drive for results they unjustifiably take over the personal responsibility of the single man or woman to make a free choice of a life partner. Since the operation of a marriage bureau must be confidential, there is no control through publicity. The chance of improper intervention in the lives of others is high. Although some bureaus are not guilty of such practices, the profit motive has changed the service into a business, and the demand for results provokes insufficient care for the responsibility entrusted them. Moreover, a further result of the operation of a bureau for profit is that the rates are too high for many single persons.

When the church finds, as did the Hervormde Kerk, that the existing means of finding a mate are insufficient or unreliable, she has an obligation to help single people supply their need. The church may never be satisfied simply with the recognition of need; she must seek to fill it. What does it profit "if a brother or sister is ill-clad and in lack of daily food, and one of you says to them, 'Go in peace, be warmed and filled,' without giving them the things needed for the body?" [17] Christian love demands that the church help unmarried persons as well as those in financial need or those needing psychic or physical care. The organization and operation of a marriage bureau by the church is not essentially different from her organization and operation of hospitals, mental institutions, orphanages, and homes for the aged. Not only Christian love but also the church's ministry demands her involvement. Since God works organically through her and since he works organically upon the individual person, the church must see that every obstacle to the life of full devotion and full service is removed. When an unfulfilled need exists in society, as a hindrance to realizing the Christian life, the church's responsibility to Christ demands efforts to supply the need.

The marriage bureau need not be organized and controlled by the offices of the church. The ministry of the church is the concern and duty of all believers. The operation of such an agency is part of their ministry to fellow believers. It can be instituted as a private, separate organization for the promotion of the ministry of the church to the older unmarried.

In such a bureau the spiritual welfare of the persons seeking aid

---

[16]   Such advertisements are common European practice. A large Dutch newpaper has as many as fifty such advertisements per day.

[17]   James 2 : 15, 16.

is of primary importance. As Smelik says of the Hervormd Huwelijks-contact bureau, the aim is "zuiver pastoraal." [18] A bureau of this kind takes into account more than just the psychic, social, and economic interests of its clients. Their religious life is of first concern. For example, admission to the correspondence circle of the Hervormd Huwe-lijks-contact bureau, through which the early contacts are made, is open chiefly to members of the Nederlandse Hervormde Kerk and secondly, in a limited measure, to members of other Christian churches. Un-believers and those who are members of no church are excluded. [19] Implicitly, this bureau reckons with the admonition of Paul, "Do not be mismated with unbelievers." [20] The membership of the governing board of this bureau also reflects its pastoral aim. It consists of a profes-sor, a psychiatrist, a medical doctor, a minister, a minister's wife, and an ecclesiastical office holder. [21] It is of great importance that an organ-ization which actively intervenes in a matter of such significance as marriage operates according to Christian principles and with a conscious-ness of the spiritual welfare of its clients. Such a method of operation is added reason for the existence of a special bureau instituted by believers.

The objections raised against the institution of the Hervormd Huwe-lijks-contactbureau are probably typical of those which would be raised in any Reformed church. They should be considered here since they question the legitimacy of such an organization. [22] Some objections are directed against the church's operation of such a bureau. These have already been considered. Others are directed against a marriage bureau per se, against organized intervention in the process of finding a mate. Some feel that organized intervention is artificial, forced, and in op-position with the essence of contact between the sexes; that it makes the finding of a mate a cold, objective business. [23] Ruitenberg rightly characterizes this as a romantic objection and admits that some romance may be lost but does not see its loss as an important objection. C. H. Meijer, writing on the same subject, remarks that romantic love has been given an improper value. It has been incorrectly placed above human sensibility. [24] Nowhere in the New or Old Testament does romantic love have the absoluteness that modern man gives it. Nor does organized intervention necessarily make an essential alteration in the

---

[18]   Op. cit., October 13, p. 153.
[19]   Hervormd Huwelijks-contactbureau, p. 4, and Smelik, op. cit., Oct. 13, pp. 153, 154.
[20]   II Cor. 6 : 14a.
[21]   Ruitenberg, op. cit., p. 510.
[22]   The objections listed in this and following paragraphs are a summary of those reported by Smelik, op. cit., pp. 157, 158; Ruitenberg, op. cit., pp. 509, 510; and C. H. Meijer, "Huwelijksbemiddeling in Nederland," Zedenopbouw, March, 1951, p. 10.
[23]   Smelik, op. cit., p. 157.
[24]   Op. cit., p. 10.

nature of the process of acquiring a mate. The Hervormd Huwelijks-contactbureau does not pair off individuals and then subtly impel them to marriage. The bureau in no way takes away the personal responsibility of the individual for his selection of a mate. The choice is entirely his. The bureau simply makes contact possible by regularly sending to all approved members lists giving a short description of all members of the other sex. Included are the age, the vocation, the social position, and other pertinent facts.

Other objections are of a more religious nature. Some oppose a marriage bureau because its operation is a human intervention into something that should be left to the providence of God. Since the Bible clearly says that God joins two people together, [25] the institution or use of any agency to reach the state of marriage shows a lack of trust in the omniscience and omnipotence of God. This objection stems from a non-Biblical concept of providence. God's providence is no blind power to which man must be only passive. God works organically in and through creation. He accomplishes his purposes through the activity of man. Any work that is done for Jesus' sake and in his name is a work of his hand. The usual way of finding a mate through ordinary social contact and dating does not differ essentially from the use of a marriage contact bureau. Both are intentional human activities.

The Bible even has an example of marriage meditation. When no wife could be found for Isaac in the land of Canaan, Abraham sent his servant Eliezer to his homeland to select one and bring her back. [26] And, significantly, although Eliezer had the direct guidance of God in the selection, he watched carefully how she conducted herself in her work by the well and inquired about her family heritage.

Marriage meditation is a legitimate and proper activity of the body of believers. When other agencies and means are insufficient or unreliable in their methods and practices, the body of Christ is impelled by her love and by her concern for effective ministry to the older unmarried, to organize a marriage bureau. The bureau should not attempt to help all other unmarried solve the problems of their singleness through marriage. On the contrary, it should see its first task as bringing each applicant to a conscious, responsible decision about whether they should remain single for the service of the Lord or whether they should marry. Secondly, this agency and its advisors and interviewers should consider as part of their task the ministry to those who deeply desire marriage but can find no mate, even through the agency of the marriage bureau. These must be given Paul's counsel in I Corinthians 7, that God can and must be served in every state and condition of life. [27]

A marriage contact bureau may be effective ministry to some older

---

[25]   Matt. 19 : 6.

[26]   Gen. 24.

[27]   These two elements were not found in any of the literature from the Hervormd Huwelijks-contactbureau or in any literature written by others about this bureau.

unmarried, but the church must also minister to those who do not marry. One of the most important parts of her ministry is the integration of the unmarried into the life of the church and into the lives of her members.

In the preceding chapter aloneness was found to be one of the most significant aspects of singleness. Not only is aloneness a psychic and spiritual problem in and of itself, but the social isolation of the older unmarried is again and again a contributing factor to their other personal problems. In the unmarried the process of individualization in American society has nearly reached its ultimate end: the solitary individual has become the unit of society. He stands alone in every area of life, and this solitude affects many of his personal problems.

Within marriage—as it was broadly defined in chapter three to include not only the husband-wife relationship but also that which can normally be expected of it, the parent-child relationship—adult men and woman find sustained, personal contact with individuals of different sexes, milieus, religious types, cultural backgrounds, and age groups. Sustained, personal contact with varied individuals gives birth to a communion with these multiform elements. Little or no conscious, intentional effort need be expended by the married person to find such communion. The possibility of it is already guaranteed by the previously established relationship, and the security of this relationship encourages him to drop his mask and show something of his true self. Thus he achieves genuine communion.

Such communion is needed by the older unmarried. The church of Christ is concerned that they find this kind of communion because of the pervasive influence of isolation. The church is concerned because she is anxious about every condition of the individual or society which restricts a man's full acceptance of the whole gospel and which thus inhibits his complete obedience to God's demands.

Therefore, the church must secure for the older unmarried a communion which has the quality of catholicity. To be catholic it cannot be based upon similiarity of age, social position, marital status, sex, etc. It must be based upon a relationship which transcends these differences. It must be a communion that is not restricted to occasional contacts or to certain areas of life. Communion which is temporally extensive and touches most, if not all, aspects of life will help them. Less will not.

Such communion can be had in the church. The *koinonia* of the church has two aspects: it is both a relationship and an activity. *Koinonia* means a close, strong affiliation: an association, society, bond, or community. [28] Inseparable from this element is the idea of the activity of fellowship which springs forth out of the relationship.

That new relationship which binds individual persons in the church

---

[28] Kittel, *op. cit.*, Vol. 3, p. 798.

is formed through their common new relationship to Christ. It is not based on individual characteristics. A person is neither included nor excluded because of his social position, culture, sex, or religious background from the new relationship to Christ, nor from the resultant new relationship to other believers. [29] Therefore, in the early church there were members of the household of Caesar and there were slaves; there were Greeks and Romans and there were Jews; there were the women Lydia and Priscilla as well as the men Paul and Barnabas; there was the aged apostle John as well as the young evangelist Timothy.

Through the new relationship to Christ, created through faith, all believers, whatever their differences, have become brothers. And they have become more than brothers, they have become one with each other. Paul expresses this new relationship by using the figure of a body and the various organs and limbs of that body. Together they form one whole, though each member of this whole differs from the others. Their *koinonia*-relationship is so close and so binding that Paul goes beyond the idea of familial relationships and uses the figure of an organism to give it adequate expression. [30]

The relationship in the community of believers has much in common with that in the tribe of native cultures, in which each person is not an individual in a group of individuals, who together constitute a society. Each is a part of the one whole: he is not the whole in himself. The society, his tribe, is the whole. In the church individuals do not lose their identity or their individuality, but they do lose their isolation by their incorporation into Christ.

The nature of the *koinonia*-activity is determined by the nature of the *koinonia*-relationship. The communion of the church is catholic. The new believer-believer relationship is socially, sexually, and culturally indiscriminate: so is the activity of the communion which springs out of it. It is not a communion of similarities. The whole society is enriched just through these differences. Each part serves the others precisely by virtue of his difference from them: the eye serves the foot and the foot the eye. [31] The differences are not annihilated by the *koinonia*-relationship, nor are they ignored in the *koinonia*-activity. They are relativized by the new relationship so that the extent of fellowship is not limited by these differences nor is the nature of fellowship determined by them. But neither do differences become insignificant. They are employed in the *koinonia*-activity so that each person can better enrich the other.

Such communion is eminently suitable for the older unmarried woman. Her marital status is a wall separating her from the rest of society. In the church this difference is overshadowed by a new relation-

---

29 I Cor. 12 : 12—27, Gal. 3 : 26—28, and Col. 3 : 11.

30 I Cor. 12 : 12—27 and Rom. 12 : 4, 5. Cf. E. P. Groenewald, *Koinonia (Gemeenskap) By Paulus,* Delft, W. P. Meinema, 1932, pp. 185 and. 191.

31 I Cor. 12 : 12—27.

ship which cuts through individual differences. Her difference is not ignored. It gains positive significance by becoming the means through which she can enrich the *koinonia*. Embarrassment and shame are replaced by a new purpose and sense to life. She is no longer an outcast, but a *koinonon:* a partner, one with whom the other has something in common, one with whom he has communion. [32] In the early church she too was greeted with the holy kiss as an expression of the love which bound all members. [33] The right hand of fellowship, an expression of welcome into the *koinonia* relationship and activity, was not denied her, since, as a believer, she was a member of the body of Christ. [34] In the church she finds social acceptance—an acceptance which is neither based on her marital status nor ignores it but gives it positive significance. Through this acceptance she learns to accept her singleness and her calling in life, while in the state of singleness.

In the *koinonia* of the church no one can say to another, "I have no need of you," for those who "seem to be weaker are indispensable." [35] The *koinonia* activity is not a fellowship of self-sufficient individuals but of mutual dependents. No one may refuse the help of other believers, since each member finds within the church the mutual support necessary for his healthy spiritual life. In the *koinonia* of the church the unmarried woman is indispensible, though she may seem to be the weaker.

Nor is any member of the church refused help because of differences in social standing, sex, or culture. In the society of the church the needs of others are not simply supplied; they are shared. The members commune in the needs of each other. [36] This mutual support, which is part of the *koinonia*-activity of the church, is not limited to specifically religious edification. All the needs of the saints are shared. The spiritual needs are filled by the contribution of a prayer from one, a song from another, or a prophecy, or an interpretation—as each is able. [37] The social needs are shared through the practice of hospitality. In the early church hospitality was so highly regarded that Paul singled it out as a way to share in the needs of others. [38] It was of such importance in the church that it was a requirement for the office of elder. [39]. The sharing of

---

[32]   Cf. Philemon 16, 17. Paul pleads with Philemon to take back his runaway slave Onesimus as a beloved brother and, even more, as a *koinonon*. The believer-believer relationship has undermined the discrimination which lies in the master-slave relationship. Cf. Kittel, *op. cit.*, Vol. 3, p. 808.

[33]   I Peter 5 : 14.

[34]   Cf. Gal. 2 : 9. The right hand of fellowship was denied Paul by the Christian Church in Jerusalem only until they were convinced that he was a true servant of Christ. Once convinced that the missionary to the gentiles was one with them, they received him into full fellowship.

[35]   I Cor. 12 : 21, 22.

[36]   Rom. 12 : 13. Cf. Kittel, *op. cit.*, Vol. 3, p. 808.

[37]   I Cor. 14 : 26.

[38]   Rom. 12 : 13.

[39]   I Tim. 3 : 2.

material needs is also part of the *koinonia*-activity of the church. Already early in the history of the church, almost as soon as the church was founded, believers understood that their new relationship to each other demanded a concern for each other's material welfare. [40] The *koinonia*-activity of the church reaches to every area of life. It is not limited to the activity of worship, but includes every aspect of existence. Neither is the *koinonia*-activity limited to occasional contacts or specific days or hours. It is not limited to Sundays or to the church services. The homes of believers are open for each other. Believers are hospitable seven days a week. [41]

Such communion the older unmarried woman and the older unmarried man need. Such communion overcomes their personal isolation. It depletes the force of one of their strongest motivations for sexual contact with others, brings them to an acceptance of self with all its conditions, and helps prevent the development of an egocentric life. In *koinonia* they learn what love is, both by receiving it and by giving it. Such communion provides the atmosphere in which the older unmarried person can come to full aceptance of the whole gospel and to a life completely devoted to God's service.

If the church is genuine church, if her life is a valid expression of her nature, if she is true to her New Testament heritage, then the older unmarried will find in her the communion they need. But mutual love, fellowship, concern, and service are no automatic result of the establishment of the new relationship. Just as the husband must be commanded to love his wife, [42] so the children of God must be exhorted to "love one another with brotherly affection." [43] The older unmarried do not, in fact, always find in the historical church, communion of the quality

---

[40] Although the community of goods described in Acts 2 : 44, 45 and Acts 4 : 32—35 was only a temporary phenomenon, the sharing of goods continued. They provided for their own who were in need (Acts 6 : 1—6 and I Cor. 16 : 1—3), they sent gifts to the poorer churches (Rom. 15 : 25, 26 and Acts 11 : 29), and they supported Paul in his missionary journeys (Phil. 4 : 15). This last text is especially significant since in it Paul specifically refers to the sharing of material things as a *koinonia*.

[41] The temporal extent of the *koinonia*-activity of the early church is evidenced by the practice of eating the evening meal together (Acts. 2 : 42, 46). This breaking of bread was very probably a real meal—although it may also have included the sacrament of the Lord's Supper—for Paul admonished the church because some go hungry at these common meals (I Cor. 11 : 21, 22). These meals were *koinonia*-activity, expressing the unity of believers, for Paul wrote the Corinthians that the reason for the degeneration of the common meals from their original character as a feast of love was that the communion had broken down through divisions among them. He added, that while such a state existed, they could better quit (I Cor. 11 : 18—23). Cf. also A. B. MacDonald, *Christian Worship in the Primitive Church*, Edinburgh, T. and T. Clark, 1934, pp. 124, 125 and pp. 133—137, where he describes these meals against the background of Jewish custom.

[42] Eph. 5 : 25.

[43] Rom. 12 : 10.

and quantity that the new relationship demands. They often find an abstract concern for others—a concern for the foreign mission field but none for the neighbor. They need a concern that is concrete and specific. They often find a limited concern—a concern only for the overtly religious life. They need the perceptive, all-compassing concern of a husband for his wife and of a parent for his child. They often find a communion whose boundaries follow the general patterns of society: the married with the married, the young with the young, etc. They need a communion which transcends these patterns.

There are dangers in integration, dangers which the church must clearly see. If, for example, the single woman finds complete social acceptance in the homes of the married, either she or the man of the household may be tempted to sexual sins. By comparison to his wife the single woman may seem to have greater freedom of activity, more money for good grooming and good clothes, and a more cultural and exciting life. There is also the danger of jealousy. The single woman may become jealous of the married woman with her husband and family; the married woman may become jealous of the single because of real or imagined attempts to attract the husband. The situation is the same for the unmarried man. He can be a temptation for those into whose lives he has been accepted, or he can be tempted by them. The church must see the dangers of integration, but she must not hold back. She must not let fear force her to choose the easy way out: *apartheid*.

To help the older unmarried the church must promote a *koinonia-activity* which is an accurate reflection of the *koinonia*-relationship. In her preaching, her catechism, and her ministry to the individual the church must clearly proclaim the significance of the one body. *Koinonia* must be as serious a matter to her as it was to Paul in his letters to the Corinthian Church. The first injunction of the first epistle (I Cor. 1 : 10) and the last of the second (II Cor. 13 : 11) was: Unity must be restored.

The task of the church in the integration of the older unmarried into her *koinoia* includes the following elements. She must make the proclamation that, however significant marriage may be, the unmarried state is not in any way contemptible. The church can proclaim this truth directly and indirectly. She proclaims indirectly by applying her general proclamation of the gospel to the unmarried as well as to the married, by choosing explanatory examples in the sermon from the unmarried life as well as from the family life, and by remembering in her public prayers the needs, blessings, and services of the unmarried as well as of the married. Thus she breaks through common prejudices; she shows that the unmarried also belong to life; she reveals an appreciation for the unmarried and their honor; she shows that she does not regard them, first of all, as failures, as those who would rather have married; she makes explicit her readiness to welcome them into full fellowship.

Secondly, the church must begin to effect integration, the necessity of which she proclaims. More pastoral calls by the minister, elders, and deacons are not the answer. Such contact is part of the official life of the church, not part of the daily life of her members. The older unmarried feel that the visits are made because the office demands it, not because the office holders have any personal interest. Also, such contact is only occasional; it is not sustained. Nor are separate societies or clubs for the older unmarried the answer. Such organizations may have some slight value as "marriage bureaus" since they provide contact with other unmarried people of the same age, but they have little value as means of integrating the single into the *koinonia* of the church; they are like little ghettos within the society of the church. If the church would learn to accept the unmarried as brothers and sisters in Christ, such separate organizations would be superfluous.

A prëeminent way to full integration is integration in the *diakonia* element of communion. The church must not only serve the older unmarried in their needs, but she must also allow them the opportunity for service of others. Because they are unmarried, they can serve in ways that others cannot. They have no family demands upon their time and attention. However, their service must not be confined to that in the choir or Sunday School. Their service must be daily service in common life.

For example, one of the ways in which the unmarried can be included in the service aspect of communion in daily life is the formation of local workgroups. K. Dijk has correctly made the point that all the members of the church, women as well as men, must be active in the ministry of the church. [44] The local workgroup—as described by R. Schippers in two articles in the *Diaconaal Correspondentieblad* [45]—is admirably suitable for the activation of the whole congregation and thus for the integration of the unmarried in the *diakonia* aspect of communion.

The church must do much social work to fulfill her ministry. Such work is more the task of the church as organism than of the church as institute [46] and therefore can best be carried out through the organization of believers into independent, local workgroups. These groups can determine what must be done and how the individual believer can help do it; they can implement on the local level the aims of all the agencies and bureaus organized for specific social purposes; they can adjust social methods and techniques to their own localities and thus avoid estranging some members of the church and endangering their spiritual welfare; and they can minister in every area of life and work at all kinds of social problems because of their free form of organization. [47] A few examples of the problems on which the local group can

---

[44]   *De Dienst der Kerk,* Kampen, J. H. Kok, 1952, pp. 249, 250. In this same context Dijk gives Scriptural support for a more extensive employment of women in the spiritual ministry as well as the material service of the church.

[45]   "Lokale Werkgroepen," Jan., 1958, pp. 3–6; Feb., 1958, pp. 23–25.

[46]   *Ibid.,* p. 3.

[47]   *Ibid.,* pp. 4–6.

work are marital adjustments, family adjustments, adjustment to unchangeable situations or conditions, choice of school or vocation, and the needs of the aged, the blind, and the invalid. The older unmarried are highly fitted for such ministry because of their freedom from social and family ties. They can give what the local workgroup demands: that they make the workgroup their permanent address. And the workgroup can give them what they demand: integration into the daily *koinonia* of the church.

Besides ministering through the marriage contact bureau and through integration into the life of the congregation and of the rest of society, the church must minister to the older unmarried through the pastoral conversation. [48] The essence and form of the pastoral conversation have been adequately described by E. Thurneysen, [49] E. L. Smelik, [50] and J. G. Fernhout. [51] Its specific content with respect to the older unmarried has been stated in those sections of chapter three which give the church's answers to their personal problems. Only a few additional remarks are necessary concerning the use of the pastoral conversation for the older unmarried.

The *koinonia* of the church is the *sine qua non* for the pastoral conversation. When two persons regard each other no longer as separate individuals but as integral parts of the same whole—the body of Christ; they can lay bare their souls to each other. The congregation creates in this world the climate in which the ministering conversation can occur. Psychologically, the unity of the saints makes possible free, uninhibited conversation because it creates the love and trust requisite for the revelation of the true self, no matter how unattractive that self may be. Therefore, the pastoral conversation becomes an effective form of ministry to the older unmarried only when that group has been integrated into the congregation and its life.

Secondly, catharsis is an especially valuable method for the conversational ministry to the older unmarried. Psychology discovered long ago that most, if not all, action is purposeful. The aim of the pastoral conversation is not to find out which commandments were broken and how often, but to discover what motivated the person to sin and what is his attitude or reaction to this sin. In the sexual problems of the single person and in his problem of acceptance of self, unconscious or semiconscious motivations often play a large role. Through the cathartic method of open, uninhibited expression of attitudes, feelings, thoughts,

---

[48] The word "pastoral" in this term describes the nature of the conversation, not the person conversing. It does not, therefore, limit this form of ministry to one or more of the special offices of the church. The word "ministerial" will be used in the same sense.

[49] *Die Lehre von der Seelsorge*, pp. 87—154.

[50] *Het Gesprek in de Pastorale Theologie*, inaugural oration, Nijkerk, G. F. Callenbach, 1949.

[51] *Psychotherapeutische Zielzorg*, pp. 125—130.

and desires, the hidden motivations can be discovered. But care must be taken that nothing blocks the free expression. No analysis, judgment, or advice may be given. The only verbal response to be given to the single person at this stage of the pastoral conversation is questions to stimulate and direct the conversation and to clarify prior statements. Although there is no general agreement upon the nature of the psychic mechanism involved, the recognition and verbal expression of desires, feelings, and attitudes often diminishes their force and annihilates the compulsion of the needs, without any solution having been found or any advice given. [52]

In the pastoral conversation with many older unmarried who have sexual problems, the use of the cathartic method is neither necessary nor advisable. Direct mention or explicit discussion of sexual problems may break communication. The sex life is so intimate and personal that an indirect approach to its problems can often be more effective. The person who enters heart and soul into the situation of the unmarried man and woman, who shows genuine Christian sympathy and understanding, who encourages them in their efforts to live the Christian life in spite of tremendous difficulties; this person has done much to strengthen their resistence to sexual temptations—even though the sexual desire was never mentioned by name. Sexual problems can be handled indirectly by placing them in the larger context of the proper attitude to all physical and psychic desires which, because of particular circumstances, are unsatisfied; or in the context of the Christian's duty to use all things in service of God: physical beauty, personality traits, physical and psychic desires, social circumstances, etc. However, when the single person himself brings up the problem or when indirect discussion is ineffective—as it is, for example, when the person has neurotic tendencies—the cathartic method can be a very valuable means of ministry.

Thirdly, in the pastoral conversation—especially when the cathartic method is being used—there is danger of transference. Every person has certain personality traits and patterns of behavior, which do not change in the pastoral conversation. Hidden desires and inhibitions will cause much the same reactions in the pastoral conversation as those in any other emotionally similar situation. [53] The intimacy, privacy, and personal quality of the pastoral conversation creates the ideal climate for the stimulation and expression of hidden desire. The danger of transference is particularly real in the conversation with the older unmarried, since they have many unsatisfied desires. For example, they may direct their sexual desires to the person guiding the conversation. The very process of thinking and speaking about sexual matters can be

---

[52] For a further description of catharsis and its use in the church's ministry, cf. C. W. Du Boeuff and P. C. Kuiper, *Psychotherapie en Zielzorg*, Utrecht, E. J. Bijleveld, 1950, pp. 93—96 and Fernhout, *op. cit.*, pp. 125—130.
[53] Cf. Horney, *op. cit.*, p. 163 and Fernhout, *op. cit.*, p. 130.

a sexual stimulant, especially when these matters are not discussed objectively—as a theoretical or scientific question—but subjectively— as a problem in which one or both of the conversers are involved. [54] For the unmarried woman there is additional cause for emotional involment and sexual desires. Since she receives the scorn of society because of her marital status, any sympathetic approach which honors her as a complete person is a powerful attractive force. The person who so approaches her becomes the object of her hidden desires.

The emotional reaction is not, however, one-sided. The person guiding the pastoral conversation also experiences a deeply emotional tie because he has become personally involved in the conflicts and problems of the unmarried person. He does not hold himself aloof from these problems and function only as a sounding board to help the single person analyze his own problems and find his own solutions. Rather, the person seeking to help the unmarried makes the problems his own. The one ministering must be doubly careful if he also has unsatisfied sexual longings, for unconsciously or semiconsciously he may be encouraging the sexual attraction and stimulating the desire. [55]

Finally, those ministering to the older unmarried in the pastoral conversation must be aware of typical spiritual dangers facing this group. In reaction to singleness the unmarried may restrict their lives to a refined culture of self: good food, a beautiful apartment, extensive vacations, the latest and best literature, the newest developments in the arts, etc. Or, they may develop a deeply rooted animosity against society because they feel they have failed while inferiors succeeded. Or, their animosity may be directed against God: they feel that he is responsible for their singleness. Again, they may deliberately seek to bring others into sexual temptation by playing the coquette or the Don Juan. Self-pity and a headlong search for entertainment and amusement are other possible reactions to singleness. The reactions to singleness—as to any other condition of man—are widely varied. [56] Because of the widespread influence of these reactions upon the spiritual life, the problem of acceptance of singleness is one of the major items to be discussed in the pastoral conversation. All spiritual resistance and animosity must be overcome, whether directed against God or against society. Friction with society is often rooted in animosity against God. The person fears to express consciously his accusation of injustice against God, so he punishes society instead. Although the unmarried person may rightly feel that *his* singleness is unpleasant and may legitimately desire to change his marital status, he must at the same time learn to accept singleness as a condition which God in his infinite love and wisdom has allowed and as a condition which can be used for God's service.

---

[54] Cf. van Andel-Ripke, *De Moeilijkste Jaren,* pp. 141, 142.
[55] *Ibid.*
[56] Cf. chapter 3 in which these and other dangers are described.

The church of Christ can minister effectively to the older unmarried through her proclamation of judgment upon social attitudes, patterns, evaluations, and premises; through the integration of the older unmarried into the church comunity and into the rest of society; through a marriage bureau; and through the pastoral conversation. However, these forms of ministry demand the activation of the whole membership of the church. Her ministry is incomplete with less.

SELECTED BIBIOGRAPHY

Bladergroen, Wilhelmina A. J., "De Werkende Vrouw Boven 30 Jaar," *Mens en Onderneming,* Vol. 7, 1953, pp. 352–367.

Deegan, Dorothy Yost, *The Stereotype of the Single Woman in American Novels,* New York, King's Crown Press, 1951.

Deutsch, Helene, *The Psychology of Women,* 2 vols., London, Research Books Ltd., 1947.

Dronkert, K., *Het Huwelijk in het Oude Testament,* Leiden, A. W. Sijthoff, 1957.

Fernhout, J. G., *Psychotherapeutische Zielzorg,* published thesis, Free University of Amsterdam, 1950.

Fry, Margery, *The Single Woman,* London, Delisle, 1953.

Groenewald, E. P., *Koinonia (Gemeenskap) by Paulus,* Delft, W. D. Meinema, 1932.

Hamer, B. Chr., *Zielzorg en Psychiatrie,* Kampen, J. H. Kok, 1952.

Harding, Mary Esther, *The Way of All Women,* New York, Longmans, Green and Company, 1933.

Herfst, J. W., "De Ongehuwde Vrouw," *Wending* (July/August, 1954), Vol. 9, Nos. 5/6, pp. 384–391.

Hohman, Leslie B. and Bertram Schaffner, "The Sex Lives of Unmarried Men,"*American Journal of Sociology* (May, 1947), Vol. 52, No. 6, pp. 501–507.

Homes, N. J., *De Vrouw in de Kerk,* Franeker, T. Wever, 1951.

Hutton, Laura, *De Ongehuwde Vrouw,* Amsterdam, Andries Blitz, [n.d.].

Klein, Viola, *The Feminine Character,* London, Kegan Paul, 1946.

Kooistra, Remkes, *De Gereformeerde Theoloog en de Sociologie,* Franeker, T. Wever, 1955.

Laurence, John, *The Single Woman,* New York, Duell, Sloan, and Pearce, 1952.

Lugtigheid, G. (ed.), *Man en Vader,* Zwolle, La Rivière en Voorhoeve, 1953.

Mead, Margaret, "Women's Social Position," *The Journal of Educational Sociologie* (April, 1944), Vol. 17, No. 8, pp. 453–462.

Neville-Rolfe, Sybil (ed.), *Sex in Social Life,* London, Allen and Unwin, 1949.

Piper, Otto, *The Christian Interpretation of Sex,* New York, Charles Scribner's Sons, 1955.

— *Het Geslachtsleven, Zijn Betekenis en Zijn Geheim,* Utrecht, E. J. Bijleveld, 1937.

Premsela, B., *De Ongehuwde Man,* Amsterdam, Andries Blitz, [n.d.].

Reik, Theodor, *A Psychologist Looks at Love*, New York, Farrar and Rinehart, 1944.

— *Of Love and Lust*, New York, Farrar, Straus, and Cudahy, 1957.

Schippers, R., *De Gereformeerde Zede*, Kampen, J. H. Kok, 1955.

Smith, M. B., *The Single Woman of Today*, London, Watts and Company, 1951.

Stern, Erich, *Die Unverheirateten*, Stuttgart, Ferdinand Enke, 1957.

Thurneysen, Eduard, *Die Lehre von der Seelsorge*, Zollikon-Zurich, Evangelischer Verlage A.-G., 1957.

Verduin, Leonard, "Toward a Theistic Evolution," *The Reformed Journal* (October, 1956), Vol. 6, No. 9, pp. 6–9; (November, 1956), Vol. 6, No. 10, pp. 9–13.

Waterink, Jan, *Plaats en Methode van de Ambtelijke Vakken*, Zutphen, Nauta, 1923.

Wyngaarden, H. R., *Gesprekken met Uzelf*, Utrecht, E. J. Bijleveld, 1955.

— *Hoofdproblemen der Volwassenheid*, Utrecht, E. J. Bijleveld, 1950.